PRAISE for *Th...*

The Right Start *is an excellent read and thought provoking for every new employee, and for many of the employees who have been around for a few years as well in the corporate world.*

Harrison and Heart worked for me for many years and they learned how to be great employees and successfully climbed the ladder. And yes, they learned the hard way.

It's a great book.

—Murli Tolaney
former Chairman and CEO, MWH Global

No book has all the answers and everyone must chart their own course, but The Right Start *should be on your reading list if you are looking to launch a successful corporate career. I know that one of the authors oversaw billion dollar projects both domestically and internationally. That's a successful career and this is exactly the guy you want to get advice from.*

—Dr. Ryan Delamater,
Founder/Pastor
OCN WTR

Packed with humorous anecdotes, this book tackles the perennial challenges every employee faces—understanding your boss, achieving work-life balance, standing out from the crowd, balancing ambition and patience, learning effective teamwork and leadership skills, and more. Recommended reading for anyone who wants to thrive in their career!

—Brad Karsh, CEO/Founder JB Training Solutions,
author *Manager 3.0.: A Millennial's Guide to Rewriting the Rules of Management*

THE
RIGHT
START

Build Your Brand to Survive and Thrive in Corporate America

DAVID HARRISON | SIMON HEART

HUGO HOUSE PUBLISHERS, LTD.

ISBN: 978-1-948261-35-7

Library of Congress Control Number: 2020906837

Cover Design and Interior Layout: Ronda Taylor, heartworkcreative.com

Hugo House Publishers, Ltd.
Denver, CO • Austin, TX
www.HugoHousePublishers.com

Dedication

To our wives: thank you for your love,
patience, and encouragement.

To our children: may you survive and thrive
in the journeys of your lives and careers.

Contents

Introduction

You Got the Job—Now What?

YOU GOT THE JOB! YOU ARE OFFICIALLY NOW PART OF THE WORK-A-DAY world in that gigantic entity known as corporate America. Congratulations!

To celebrate, we've written this book because, well, it's all about you. It's always been about you. It's how you have always lived your life; there's nothing necessarily wrong with that approach.

Sadly, it doesn't really port over to the working world.

The corporate world—the world in which you will work for a long period of time—is not about you. It's not about meeting your needs, satisfying your desires, promoting your social values, or helping you recycle used (and rare) Brazilian hardwoods. The You in the corporate world refers almost exclusively to what You can do for "Them." In this case, Them refers to your company, your boss, your team, your customers, the shareholders, and pretty much anyone else who has a stake in your company and what you do for your company. In short, it's every entity *besides* you. Thus, it's not so easy keeping the rugged individualist thing going when you go to work for a big organization.

But here's the big secret that those who ultimately thrive learn fairly early on: You and Them are not mutually exclusive. There is an intersection; some "us" exists in the working world. It's that simple and yet that difficult because You and Them are complex, dynamic, irrational, demanding, self-centered, egotistical, and sometimes very decent living organisms.

The Framework

We've learned over the years that the most effective processes have a framework (we are engineers, after all). So to help you successfully create and navigate the "us," through your career, we've put together a framework for you to help you recognize that you can still be You and that, for the purposes of career success, you can adapt You into a person that doesn't just survive but thrives in both the corporate world and in the remainder of your existence as well.

The first step is to do the hard work to discover who you really are. You can figure out things you'd like to learn and ways that you'd like to behave and head down those trails. You can learn how to work with your boss and your team. You can learn how to deliver great work products and you can develop the personal skills that are required to become a leader. This is the You we want to explore with, well … *you!*

We want you to be smart about recognizing the signals that are opportunities to shine. It starts with your first day on the job, and these signals will continue throughout your career.

Right now, you're in survival mode. You may or may not have experienced your first day. If you haven't, know that your first task is to get oriented. Start getting to know people right away. Find out what your working hours really are (not just what's posted), where the coffee machine is located, and when you can take lunch. You will meet with a Human Resources representative who will help you to understand the insurance benefits and sign up for life insurance that you hope you never need.

Part of survival mode is figuring out what you need to do to get along with people, do the things that are required of you, and hopefully make a positive impression on the people that matter (whoever they may be because outside of your boss, you really aren't too sure who really matters in your organization).

You'll feel pretty comfortable in a matter of months, perhaps even weeks. To us, that's a *big* caution sign, because we've found over the years that your first sense of "comfort" is a result of not fully understanding yourself in the working world and not fully understanding the organization for which you work. You need to get this understanding to survive—and that brings us back to the framework. This is how it goes:

In the beginning, it really is all about you. You need to understand who you are before you can figure out how you fit into the organization. This might take some introspection which, we all know, can be a bit scary. It will, however, be worth the pain to better understand who you are—BUT, we're not done here yet. The next step is actually striving to be yourself and to manage yourself *within the context of your corporate organization*. No matter what you do or where you work, getting a better understanding of You is something worth doing and we strongly encourage you to do just that.

Once you have You figured out a little better, then you need to shift gears to the part where it's about "them." You've got to take that You and figure out how to get along with your boss, work with your boss, and deliver for your boss. Success in this area comes out of the "school of hard knocks." You'll take a few gut punches before you really figure this out. To turn those gut punches into love taps, you'll need to put some effort into both understanding your boss and figuring out how you can best work with your boss.

You'll also be part of a team in your corporate organization. This becomes another type of Them that you need to figure out. We want you to understand what it takes to get along with your team, work with your team, and help your team be successful. This is an area where your behavior, work ethic and flexibility set you apart from every other cubicle Hobbit in your company. It's never easy, as teammates come in all sizes, shapes, and levels of intelligence.

You'll find that the team dynamic can make some people easier to deal with and turn some people into Orcs who are perpetually having a bad day (staying with the *Lord of the Rings* theme). We want you to know how to handle the situations that are likely to arise; ranging from when your team is celebrating a great success to that time around 11 p.m. when one or more of the team members hops on the Crazy Train. You can be the adult in the room. Trust us on this one—you really want to be the adult in the room.

However, at some point, you're going to want to move away from survive and find ways to thrive in your career. You want to make a difference in this world. Spoiler alert here: You can't change corporate to create the global view you desire. You probably can't change corporate at all until you become the boss (and even then, corporate change is an ethereal thing that has more of an existence in textbooks than it does in the real world). Notwithstanding this very unfortunate bit of news, there are ways to thrive.

It starts with delivery. We want you to learn how to deliver what you promise. First, you must learn what you are capable of doing so you can make promises that can realistically be kept. Then, you need to use readily available tools and develop the skill sets that can help you and your team deliver excellence to your boss, your company, your clients, the shareholders—whomever it is. You begin to thrive when you become known as the person who can deliver.

Those who deliver get the chance to lead. In most cases, people who really know how to deliver have some leadership skills. You can really thrive in your organization when you carefully assess where you are as a leader and then undertake to get better at those specific leadership skills and behaviors that you lack. You don't have to speak like Winston Churchill, have the organizational skills of Nancy Pelosi, or the vision of Steve Jobs to be a great leader. You simply need to understand what it takes to inspire others and to communicate your inspirational message to others in a way that gets them to do what you need them to do to be successful. It's sometimes easy and sometimes hard to do that, but our job is to help you get there.

It's YOUR Career

There's so much that goes into your work life. Your career defines a large part of who you are. And the most important thing to understand about your career path is that no one cares more about it than you. In fact, other than your parents, your significant other and maybe a few friends, no one really cares about your career. Why is that? Well, you know that people who love you and care about you also want you to be happy, and they understand that since you spend at least eight hours a day at work, that this is a big part of your happiness.

On the other hand, while your mentor, your boss, and maybe the nice HR person who says hello to you at the neighborhood coffee shop on the weekends wants you to be successful, they are more worried about their own careers and happiness and just don't have enough energy to worry about you at the same level.

Your career is your responsibility. You will, for the most part, create your own level of "luck." You are the one that will make the choices that impact your career and you should recognize, starting now, that most choices you make will have an impact on your career.

That's why this book is about *You*. It's also about *Them*. It's about your company, your boss, your team, your life outside of work, and your plans to go mountain biking on Saturday. It's about how all these things go into the mixing bowl of work and life to create the corporate you that doesn't just survive but thrives. In the process we hope you find the *You* that you are looking for. Enjoy the journey!

PART ONE

SURVIVE!

ONE

Who Are You?

Discovering the Elements of Your Brand

THIS MAY BE THE SINGLE MOST IMPORTANT CONCEPT THAT COMES OUT of this book. Who are you? How would you describe yourself?

Please don't use biz-speak jargon like "hard-charger" or "self-starter." You simply should not use those clichés in a competitive business environment if you want to differentiate yourself. On the other hand, if you want to be one of the unidentifiable masses, please feel free to use these and other similar worn-out terms.

But who are you really? Sometimes we don't even know who we are outside of our avatar we created for whatever game everyone happens to be playing online at the time. In the real world, where you can't go back to your last save point, we need a healthy dose of introspection coupled with the sage and caring advice of others to help us ferret out who we are and how we can grow.

How can we do that? This is a journey that starts with you but must include others. This is where mentors come in. This is where your real close friends can help you. This is where an honest conversation with a parent or grandparent might help as well—though we would not recommend that you start there because—well, you probably know why. On the other hand, no one knows you better than your family and they probably have the guts to tell you where you have a "blind spot" in your life. It's more than that. You

1

need to have an honest conversation with yourself as to who you are both at work and outside of work. And, perhaps equally or even more importantly, how does this definition of You relate to your awesome job? How can that person bring value to your new organization?

Careers are long and winding roads. The version of word processing software will change, your boss will change, your company will change, the rules of international soccer will change, and you will change. We've divided our book into two chunks because things will—all together now—change. One of the things that will certainly change is where you are at in your career. You'll go from survival mode to thriving mode over time and the things you need to know to thrive are not necessarily critical when you are simply trying to keep your head above water. If you are in survival mode and have time to only read half the book, then read the part on survival. If you are farther along in your career, read both chunks because the concepts for thriving are additive to the concepts presented for surviving. We think that wherever you are in your career, you'll find elements of both Survive and Thrive that will directly apply to what you are doing right now. So let's get into it.

FINDING THE REAL YOU

You're awesome. If for some reason no one has ever told you that, we're telling you that right now. You bring unique and interesting skills, educational background, work experience, and life experience to your workplace. That uniqueness is awesome, *but* you need to recognize that everyone is unique and thinks of themselves as special. And they are—all of you are special. Before we explore how all of you unique people work together, we want to explore you.

GET OVER YOURSELF

• • • • •

"Humility is not thinking less of yourself,
it's thinking of yourself less."
—PASTOR RICK WARREN

So here you are, standing atop the victory of your recently acquired employment. A beautiful moment of triumph to be sure, and you must have so many questions. You are undoubtedly wondering how to best invest in a wardrobe brimming with business casual pieces, mulling over which font will suit your email signature, and considering whether or not bringing in your electric car of the month calendar will make you look like a dweeb. Free tip, it will.

You are now living in a brave new world. What you once called Guidance Counselors are now called bosses and their cold-blooded job is to get you to do stuff that includes filling out forms and watching cybersecurity videos. Everyone in "corporate" starts out in some form of semi-dronish existence while we wait for the company to get our names correctly put into their email system. This is the time you discover that you have to work with both the AARP members and those that share your taste for lemon-ginger Kombucha.

And here's another news flash: not everyone has the same world view as you. Just because you want things to be a certain way in your personal life, your sense of social justice, your language, your level of kindness, does not mean that those sensibilities can reasonably carry over into your work life. In fact, we're going to go ahead and crush your hopes: they can't. In the corporate world, no amount of HR personnel, teambuilding seminars, or workplace diversity, is going to eradicate all people who are opposed to your opinions and points of view.

We know that your views are empirically right, and everyone else's are wrong, and you need to educate them for the sake of the planet, earthlings, and members of the galactic alliance. However, the workplace is this whole new world that is *not about you*. Again, for the people in the back, the sun does not rise and set on your opinions and existence.

Therefore, you need to learn to operate in an environment that isn't built with your personal comfort in mind. So here is our sincere advice: the first thing you need to do as a newly minted corporate stiff is to let go of your self-centrism. We're not asking you to let go of your principles, or water down your beliefs, we're asking you to sand down the sharp edges. The old adage that you catch more bees with honey totally applies here, so take this as an opportunity to influence other people in a low-key long-term way rather than proselytizing on day one.

Bottom line, you are going to be living every day with people who are not like you, and you need to square yourself with that.

- Your boss is going to accidentally say something that has passed from the accepted racial vernacular,
- your cubical neighbor is going to be confrontational about easily debunked conspiracy theories
- your favorite receptionist who moonlights as a clairvoyant medium will want to do a reading for you at lunch
- the guy in the marketing department is working hard to get you into his multi-level marketing group that sells discount movie tickets …

… and you are going to need to let all of that roll off your back.

Over the years we've encountered many colleagues who we found to be, at first, very off-putting. They dressed funny, had odd hair styles, engaged in strange hobbies, and gave us unsolicited advice. Ultimately, we learned you just have to give people some space to be who they are. We stopped judging people's clothes and hair, found their strange hobbies an interesting topic for a two-minute hallway conversation, and shrugged off their advice as caring but unnecessary. Today, that "advice giver" has become a very good friend who, interestingly enough, now solicits advice from us.

Think of your workplace as this perfect place to practice a whole other level of Zen. The easiest way to do this is to give people the benefit of the doubt. All the effort you might put into judging—or loathing—someone you work with could better be put into the work that you are supposed to be doing. So figure it out, lower your expectations, be kind, pretend everyone is from a low IQ planet that you have been charged with protecting, think of Mother Teresa, say the serenity prayer, whatever it takes to get you past how badly you are bothered.

Here's the secret no one will tell you, at least to your face: you will inevitably bother someone too, so it is in your interest to give people some room. On your way to peace and goodwill toward all mankind, you will find that every time you hold back a quip or dismiss a criticism, it becomes easier and easier to do so. Prepare to be canonized. The lesson is this: the bad vibes don't last unless you let them. Blisters eventually turn into callouses. Wine gets better with time. The guy who works across the hall and eats a disturbing amount of sunflower seeds during the Monday morning staff meeting will become a valued colleague.

I GOTTA BE ME

· · · · ·

"To thine own self be true, and it must follow,
as the night the day, thou canst not
then be false to any man."

—WILLIAM SHAKESPEARE

When the Chairman of the Board (I'm talking about Sinatra here) sang "I Gotta Be Me," he was talking about being himself in all situations—for better and for worse. You gotta be you. When you try to be something that you are not, or someone that you are not, you will ultimately be discovered and that usually ends up in a dumpster fire type situation. You have to be yourself—but we'd like to ask you two simple questions: Who are you in your everyday life outside of work and who, in the context of your job, exactly, are you? We don't pretend to be Dr. Phil, so this is no psychological exercise. It is really intended to be food for thought. Who are you AND who would you like to be? And can you get to where you'd like to go?

You are who you are. Think about it. If you are a great writer, you're a great writer. If you are naturally a goofball, you're a goofball. A leader, then a leader; a wallflower, then a wallflower; a liar, then a liar. That's a bit harsh, you say. "Yeah, I may stretch the truth from time to time, but am I liar?" Well, maybe.

We would like to point out to you that you probably don't really know who you are. Most people don't because it takes a bit of introspection along with some frank and blunt discussion with the people who know you the best to figure out who you really are. Most people, unfortunately, don't really like what they discover. We are selfish creatures who usually do what we think benefits ourselves the most. This could be lying, joking, writing, following, or leading as our own skills and personality drive our actions. If we are really honest with ourselves, we are often chameleons who change and adapt ourselves as a function of our environments: one person at the club, another person when we are with our significant other's parents, and someone completely different at work.

Okay, you're probably a pretty decent person and you most assuredly have some outstanding qualities that are of great benefit to society, your company, your clients, your family, friends, and colleagues. So, be honest and figure out the "good you" and the "not-so-good" you.

So let's look at who you are—the good things mostly. Figure out how you can apply the "good you" to the benefit of your clients, your company, and your career.

David gives a great example of this: "I am an optimist by nature. I tend to see the silver lining in every cloud and the opportunity in every problem. It is an immutable part of my nature for better and for worse. I will tell a client that I can fix a project delivery problem. I'll tell the client how I will work to fix the problem and when I will fix the problem, and then I will roll up my sleeves and work with the project team to fix the problem. I'm always optimistic that every problem is an opportunity. When we deliver, then it's good optimism. When we don't, then I'm a bad optimist.

"Sadly, I'm a bad optimist more often than a good optimist. I now recognize that I need to be very careful about what I promise to our clients, what I promise to my team, and what I promise to my family. Optimism is great, but it's far better when tempered with realism. Optimism isn't evil, nefarious, or inherently bad in any way. It's simply a part of who I am that I know I need to temper with realism. This took me more than twenty years to figure out."

There is good news for the "not-so-good" you. *You* can change. You work to be who you would like to be. Maybe you'll never be a great golfer, a Grammy-winning musician, a brilliant inventor, or a peerless leader, but you can work to improve yourself in specific aspects of your behavior and affect. David can modify his behavior and become more of a "realistic optimist." The great news is that your brain can "re-wire" itself and you can, to a reasonable extent, modify your behavior.

By way of warning, this is not a Victor Frankenstein-esque transformation. You probably can't bring something to life that doesn't exist. I will never play the guitar like Stevie Ray Vaughan despite my vast stores of optimism. If you are a shrinking wallflower, you may not be able to get all the way to the fearlessness of Forrest Gump, but you can absolutely get much better and certainly get markedly better.

This takes two things: desire and effort. You have to want to get better and you have to work at it. Make yourself a list and pick one or two areas that you will focus on for improvement: not three, not five—one or two. Then every day remind yourself of these areas and work on them at every opportunity. It need not be complex, and you shouldn't have to get a licensed therapist to help you. If you do feel like a licensed therapist can help you, then by all means, go see one.

For David, these two areas were very different. "I am one of those resting frowny face people. In fact, I've been rightfully accused of having 'resting really angry face.' I may look like I'm not happy all the time, but I'm truly a happy person most of the time. I need to remind myself constantly to smile. I want to retrain my face muscles to smile rather than frown. The second thing I need to remind myself daily is to listen more than I talk. I've come up with a methodology to help me do this. I always ask colleagues, clients, my boss, about a topic of interest to them which includes, in no particular order, their kids, movies they've seen, books they are reading, etc. The point is to get them talking about themselves and their interests, *and* I try to never follow that up with a conversation about me. They talk and I listen (more on this in the 'Tell Me About Yourself,' section below). I'm working on rewiring my brain, and when I get better in those two areas, I'll work on some of my deeper personality disorders."

Who would you like to be? Let's look at this in two ways—skills and behavior. You have to be realistic about skills. You can't get the superpowers of a comic book hero without the inherent angst, an unfortunate laboratory accident involving neutrinos, immense wealth, or magic. You can't sing like Lady Gaga without some God-given talent that, let's face it, you probably don't have. But you can learn skills. You can learn to sing, and you'll sing at your own personal best when you practice daily (I believe showers were initially invented to enable you to practice your singing skills).

You can gain a deeper understanding of the various varieties of salt that exist in the culinary universe and become an expert on the integration of *Fiore de Cervia* (a very fancy salt) and Italian Kale if you determine that this is something you'd like to study. You can learn to be a better speaker, and you'll get to a pretty decent level when you practice, practice, practice. You can learn about different aspects of your business; you can learn more about your clients and customers so that you can better serve them; you can learn how to read the financial spreadsheets that only the CFO really seems to understand; you can learn the jargon of the IT folks so you can have a real conversation with them. The path to success in all these skills has two common elements—desire and effort. Enough said.

Skills can be defined in many ways in a business context. You understand your company and your business (or maybe you don't, and if that's the case then acquiring that knowledge should come first.) Ask your boss about skills they think you need. Ask your mentor (more on this later) about skills that were beneficial to them. Ask your foosball partner from accounting what skills they have (outside of really quick hands) that have actually helped them in their job. Think about developing business skills that would benefit your career or that you'd actually like to have. We'll have some suggestions on this as we move through the book.

You also need to think about your behaviors. This aspect of You is perhaps even more important than your list of business skills. The *YOU* reflected in your behavior is relevant both inside and outside of work. Behaviors include things that you naturally do (like laugh a lot or show empathy), and things that you decide to do (stop gossiping or taking credit for work done by others). I can't tell you how to behave. That's up to you and your roommates who want you to do your own dishes. I can simply point you in the direction of others who have thought this through. There are many, many books on this topic, but I'll just point you to one set of behavioral principles published by a guy named John Perry Barlow. He was an internet pioneer, Harvard University Fellow, and lyricist for the Grateful Dead who published a list entitled "25 Principles for Adult Behavior." It's a great list and I highly recommend it (just Google it). And I want to give a shout out to my colleague and friend, John, who shared this with our leadership team.

Who are you? Who would you like to be? What steps will you take? Start stepping.

THE WHOLE TRUTH

• • • • •

"Your time is limited, so don't waste it by living someone else's life."

—STEVE JOBS

This is a corollary to "I Gotta Be Me." You do have to be yourself, and there are aspects of yourself that you can change. The big caution here is simply this; you cannot be a phony. You can't act like you care about others when you really don't. You can't act like a great altruist when everything you do is calculated to bring attention to yourself and benefit to you. You can't act like you always say nice things about others and then go talk trash about them behind their backs.

Take David. He likes beer (and isn't that a nice way to start a paragraph). "I don't like IPAs (boo, hiss—I hear you out there). I realize that there's a wide swath of the population that are between twenty-one (legal drinking age but more likely eighteen if we take into account every college campus in the US) and eighty who love IPAs. They probably love all the various variants of IPAs that combine some type of fruit with the hops. I also like beer with clever names like 'Hoptimus Prime,' or 'Duck Duck Gooze.' It just feels good saying these words to the server, but unfortunately for me, these great names tend to be skewed mostly to IPAs. For a long time, when out for a beer after work with the "work crowd," I would order the beer with the cool name (just to be in with the "cool crowd") and not like it and, consequently, not drink it. What a dumb thing to do. The right thing is to 'be me.' I don't order the IPAs anymore and thankfully, the rest of the craft beer world has caught up, and I can now order beers that are named after me, such as 'Aging Hipster,' that you can get at the Peckish Pig in Chicago."

Life, for most people, is about more than the beer they like. It's uncomfortable and unpleasant to be a "fake-IPA-drinker." The "cool crowd" knows you're trying too hard, and you don't get the reflective positive vibe from them that you hoped to get. It takes effort to try to be something that you are not, and often it's very uncomfortable, and not very pleasant.

Cicero (a very, VERY old white guy) said *esse quam videri.* Translated this means "be rather than seem." Early in pretty much everyone's career, they strive hard to "seem" and while that may have helped them get promoted, it did not help them be successful in the jobs to which they were promoted. This is a sure-fire way to fail. Why? Simply because "seem" is not the same as "is." You cannot learn and grow when you project a false or partially false image about yourself. David said he didn't even realize that he was doing this until later in his career when he looked back and asked himself what he did wrong, and what he could have done better.

"Amongst my failure points was a lack of experience for the new position because I was faking it in some areas. I wasn't as strong of a leader as I thought I was because I didn't like controversy or debate at that point in my career. I avoided being honest with myself that I was faking it. But that was the very truth that I needed to know about myself."

Faking gets found out—maybe only by yourself—but you will have to face that truth when you don't take Cicero's advice.

Social media is a perfect place for people to *esse quam videri.* Your Facebookery skills and prowess at recording, editing, and posting Instagram videos are very impressive, but these don't describe you, *unless* you are perpetually on vacation, always eat out at Michelin-starred restaurants, or attend major sporting events three times per week. We may not be the right people to talk about how you get puppy ears on the Snapchat photo, but we do frequently flip through Instagram, Twitter, and Facebook posts from a wide variety of friends, work colleagues, and high-school acquaintances whom we've not seen in decades.

Social media is a place where you open your kimono for all to see. Sometimes it's just fine, like your four-year-old's birthday party. Sometimes, it can go horribly wrong when you decide to make political commentary, say something about your boss, criticize your company's training policies and you can fill in the blanks because you know how many things can go wrong on social media.

That said, everything that you convert into digital format and place on a social media site is something that a colleague, potential employer, or bad-guy-who-wishes-you-ill can find. Do not place (or please consider not placing) anything on a social media site that could prevent you from employment, promotion, friendships, or lead to harming or destroying your reputation. You will not regret sharing less about your life, nor should you regret sharing less about your cat.

You probably know people who do this; people who present themselves to the social-media world in a positive way when, in fact, their actions, no matter how aptly they hide them, say something else. People in the public spotlight have teams of publicists and advisors who help them craft a public persona. If that public persona isn't at least pretty close to who they really are, they get found out and the "finding out" is never good. There are so many public figures who have stumbled over the past several years that we chose to not list any specific examples. They will probably be out-of-date and out-shadowed by a whole new batch of phonies who get busted between the time we type these words and the time you read them.

You can think of athletes, musicians, politicians, religious leaders, business leaders, and government figures who have projected a certain public image of themselves only to be busted by something they have been caught doing. There are business leaders who have projected ethical images in the media and then have gone to jail for insider trading. People lie on their resumes, take credit for things that they have not done, claim skills that they do not have, and claim strong business relationships with others that are barely more than acquaintances. You get the picture. The Masquerade Ball aspect of the business world is also not limited to business—it's a reality in all aspects of our lives.

You don't have to be a player in this crazy play. You can *be* rather than *seem*. You might start with a little self-examination. Find something about yourself, something very specific to you, and ask, "Who am I kidding?" If it holds true, great. If it doesn't, then you can work to change it.

It doesn't have to be something grand like a big aspect of your personality. A former colleague claimed to be a scratch golfer. He didn't make this claim idly over lunch; he made it part of who he was. He told everyone that he was a terrific golfer. But when opportunities presented themselves for him to golf at company events, he always declined citing some physical malady such as a sore back or an upset stomach. Okay, maybe he really was a great golfer at one time in his life and Father Time, who as we all know is undefeated, had been unkind to his golf game and his body. (That would at least explain the sore back thing. We never knew why he so often had an upset stomach.)

One day, on our way to lunch, another colleague showed our "great golfer" a couple of new clubs he had just purchased. The great golfer examined the clubs, looked up at the club owner, and asked, "What does the 'S' on this club stand for?"

"Sand Wedge," replied the owner as the rest of us looked on in stunned silence.

How is it that a great golfer cannot identify a sand wedge? It's the only golf club with a *big* "S" on it. Perhaps he is not being fully truthful about his golfing prowess. And, if he is being disingenuous in this area of his life (which doesn't really matter with respect to business acumen and performance) perhaps he is also being disingenuous about his education, his background, his abilities, his business relationships. As it turns out, he was a big phony in business as well, claiming skills and business relationships he did not have. Surprise, surprise.

It's not just business acumen or athletic skills that people can "exaggerate." It can be personal stuff as well. David was working long hours in another city on a project with a team that included the President of our Division. We'd work late, have a late dinner, and return to the hotel for a drink and cigar after eating and drinking too much at dinner. The Division President and some of his acolytes liked to have a cigar with their "nightcap." He's not a cigar smoker, but he wanted to be one of the gang, so he engaged in the "puffery." On the second night, as he was puffing and drinking away, he started to feel ill and excused himself about 50 percent of the way through his drink and about 20 percent of the way through the expensive Cuban cigar that someone had given him. The next morning as the team gathered to walk to the office, the cigar smoking and nightcap drinking crowd all had a laugh at little-old-lightweight David. He acted like something he wasn't, and he got busted. Harmless fun on their part, and he deserved the friendly mockery. It was a classic case of being a phony.

Don't be a phony, don't lie, don't embellish. Just be honest.

TELL ME ABOUT YOURSELF

• • • • •

"We make a living by what we get,
we make a life by what we give."
—WINSTON CHURCHILL

Confession. The title is misleading. We're not talking about *you*. We're talking about the *other* guy.

Earlier, we mentioned the importance of getting others to talk about themselves. Here's where we expand on that idea.

There was an interview on sports radio a while back with a guy named Herman Edwards who played and coached in the National Football League for decades. He had success as both a player and a head coach, playing in one Super Bowl and coaching and winning numerous playoff games. He never won a Super Bowl as either a player or a coach. "Could you really say that you have had a successful career since you have never won the ultimate prize, the Super Bowl?" he was asked in a radio interview. "Yes," he responded emphatically. "Football was my occupation. It never defined who I am as a man." Coach Edwards then went on to briefly explain his life philosophy—how he tries to marry up words and deeds in his life as he lives it every day.

Very few people play in the NFL. Even fewer can say they have been a head coach; and yet these things don't define you as a person? How can that be? It can be because Herman Edwards is the rare individual who has carefully considered who he is, who he wants to be, and how he will live out his life in such a way that his deeds match up with his words. He opens doors for people. He doesn't use profanity ("Not in my vocabulary," he proclaims.) He considers how he is representing his employer and his profession to others; he is clear and direct with others, and he cares about making a positive impact on the lives of those with whom he works. Yup, we got all of this from an interview on sports radio.

Can you talk about your life philosophy outside of work? When someone asks you about yourself, do you respond with your occupation and nothing else or does that define you? And why would that be bad? Some employers would love it if all of their employees stated that they were defined by the company they worked for or the job that they had. Most employers, however, want well-rounded individuals. Employers want people who bring diverse life experiences to their jobs and can interact with others at multiple levels, not only in a "work context."

This is critically important in almost every profession today. You aren't dealing with people just like you who have the same life experiences, went to the same universities, and have 2.3 perfect children (on average). You must be able to work with colleagues and clients who have lives outside of work and you can only do this successfully if you, yourself, have a life outside of work that enables you to define yourself by something more than your profession.

There's another level here about self-definition that comes from Coach Edwards. If you are defined by your occupation, you'll never really be happy until you are in the top job at the biggest and most successful company in your industry. Let me repeat that: if you define yourself by your work, you'll not be happy in any job you have. You'll always say to yourself that you'll be happier when you get promoted. How do we know this? It's something we've struggled with our entire careers—many people do. "If I could just get to the next level, I'll be happier, I'll be more successful in the eyes of my friends and family, I'll have more money, I'll have/be *whatever*." It's simply not true.

People have known this and struggled with this for millennia. Yes, you are correct; that's many thousands of years. Read the first chapter of the

Book of Ecclesiastes in any version of the Bible to see what King Solomon thought about money and success thousands of years ago. We'll paraphrase it for you so you don't have to look it up: "It's all vanity, and it will all pass away." Wanting to do more in your organization is not wrong or bad. It's a good thing to want to build your skills and capabilities so that you can be promoted to a higher level, and it's a good thing to make more money because you do more for your company. But guard against it being the only thing that will make you happy in this world, because it's not.

Why do you care if one of your friends thinks you are less successful in your career because you are a Vice President and not a Senior Vice President? Will your family love you more if you are sitting in the C-suite as opposed to being a mid-level manager? The answers are that you shouldn't care what your friends think about your career, and your family will not love you any more or less as a function of your career level. David has been told by his own family that they'd be most appreciative if he'd stop answering his cell phone or responding to incessant emails while on vacation.

We decided long ago that we would always strive to do the best job we could possibly do in whatever role our company thought would best serve the organization. David always introduces himself as an engineer (even though he doesn't do much engineering anymore) and a father of four. He rarely talks about his position in the company because it's not necessary. Most of his clients that he meets know he's some kind of "big shot" with the company because he has gray hair and wears business suits. But David is very clear about this point, "I want to know that my legacy will NOT be my position with the company; rather (like Coach Edwards) I hope it will be the positive impact I have made on the many people that I work with and that work for me. This includes both clients and colleagues alike. To me there is no greater compliment than when an employee, a colleague, a peer, or a client tells me that they have learned something from me. That is the type of person I am striving to be."

People want to know who you are, but they don't always want the fun facts about your life. In the past, we have erred in giving too much information to people. We now call this TMI. (We still say that, right?) People don't want to hear about your doctor's visit, your kid's softball game, your wife's charity event, or your alarm system with twelve wireless cameras that you scored at Costco over the weekend. Those things aren't really who you are. It's fine to say you are a father or mother, a Little League coach, a team parent, a charity volunteer. It's usually best to leave it at that unless someone begs you to give them the details. This just in to the News Room: most people simply don't want to know.

On the flip side of this, we have found that when we *do* want to know, it opens the door to all those things you want in a relationship—like trust. Most people do like to talk about themselves, so we ask people to give us as much detail as they'd like. It doesn't matter that quite often they don't reciprocate. If they ask, we'll tell. If they don't want to tell us about their kids, their charity, their golf game, their moose hunting adventure—they don't have to, and we won't force them. We're always prepared when we meet someone to let them tell us about their personal lives. If they prefer to not do that, then we're prepared with current events (mostly apolitical events if possible) that we can bring up for discussion. The key is to get them talking, but don't offer up anything about yourself unless asked to do so.

David recently met with a client who is the City Engineer in a large southern California city. He's really busy, so they scheduled a thirty-minute window. The purpose of the meeting was to get feedback on David's company's performance on a large project that this individual had overseen. David walked into this guy's office and noticed he had a road bike on one wall next to a framed pictures of rock climbing and skiing adventures that he'd been on with his wife. Perfect. They talked road biking and rock climbing (even though David is not a rock climber, for the record.) Their half hour meeting stretched to about one hour. Half of it was a discussion of climbing, biking, marriage, and families. It was a great discussion. When they got down to business, they had a completely different discussion that was just as great.

How fortunate for David that his client liked stuff he liked. This was easy. If the client was interested in things that David knew nothing about, such as breeding Shetland ponies or the finer points of non-GMO pasta making, he wouldn't have minded. That's because we know the best phrase to keep a conversation going: "That's really interesting, please tell me more!"

ARE YOU A BRAND BURNER OR A BRAND BUILDER?

• • • • •

> *"A brand for a company is like a reputation for a person. You earn reputation by trying to do hard things well."*
>
> —JEFF BEZOS

Finding out who *you* are has everything to do with *your brand*. You are a brand that represents you, your company, your family, and, in some cases your favorite NFL team. (I'm looking at you, Raiders fan.)

Knowing who you are, and how people perceive you (and therefore, perceive your brand) is so much more that a phone call to a late night psycho-fixer radio show. This isn't about tearing out your soul in front of others so everyone can say something affirming. It's not about self-help books, Zen, meditation, or anything else that we might be forgetting right now. Finding you, and understanding your brand, is simply a starting point for your corporate journey, and to be honest, your life journey.

When you start a career, you need to be aware that your decisions, from how you dress to the invites to lunch you take up, or turn down—affect how others see you and thus act towards you. It's called your personal brand, and just like a company has to pay attention to how others view them as a brand, you as a person embarking on a career have to pay attention to how you present yourself to the world.

As you start really looking at *you*, think of you as a brand. However you present *you* to the world will have an impact, either positive or negative.

We've seen it happen too many times: the hard-working guy who's ambitious, smart, and wants to succeed … but who makes a mistake now and again that hurts him more than helps him.

We all make mistakes and not every mistake is going to land you in the "you're fired" category. Believe us, we've made them too. When Simon was a summer intern, the regional manager asked him to lunch. He didn't go because he had promised his supervisor (who was many rungs on the corporate ladder below said Regional Manager) that he would have a project done and delivered by that same afternoon. He later told his supervisor about declining the lunch and she laughed at his naivety. "You didn't go to lunch?! Yikes—that was not an important deadline. You could have gotten the project to me later. Just ask me next time!"

It was an instructive moment. While certainly a minor *faux pas* for Simon, he maintained his integrity and perhaps added a small brush-stroke to the personal brand picture he was starting to paint for himself as a hard worker that delivers on promises.

It is important to remember this rule: You will be known not by what you say, but by what you do. When you're presented with a choice on what to do, act, or say, ask yourself two simple questions:

Are you a brand burner?

Or a brand builder?

It's pretty easy to spot the brand builder versus the brand burner.

The employee who, within the first month of getting hired, makes last minute plans for a four-day weekend with college buddies, missing two days of work. The first real conversation with her boss was "asking" to take a couple days off, (Flights were already booked so it was more telling than asking.)

How different would this person's brand have been if the first five conversations with her boss were about figuring out ways she could best deliver value for the company, or the most important skills for her to learn sooner rather than later. Then, maybe the sixth or tenth conversation could be about taking a couple days off after some good hard months of work and giving the boss plenty of notice ahead of time.

We've seen some of the worst brand-burning moves in our collective decades of corporate experience having to do with travel—because that's the kind of company we worked for. Some are simply boneheaded, like the guy who misses his flight, and thus misses an important meeting, because he refused to throw away a 5 oz bottle of toothpaste discovered by airplane security. (He decided to get out of the security line and check his bag—why bother?)

Some simply defy any explanation, like the guy who had been asked to join his boss's boss on a trip to Dallas during his first six months with the company. He gets to the airport nice and early, but then falls asleep at the gate and never boards the plane. His boss's boss doesn't learn he is without support at the meeting until he lands in Dallas and waits for everyone to get off the plane, but no sign of our new guy. Yes, he was embarrassed, but a phone call apologizing would have done wonders.

These are simple, binary choices. If you aren't aware that your choice could have lasting positive or negative impact, you may not make the right choice. So, which brand do you want to exhibit?

- The new employee who wonders if they can get administrative log in rights for their lap top so they can load games that they will play "during their breaks."
- The employee who gets frustrated one day and decides to post a "my company sucks" diatribe on social media complete with a #mycompany and another #mycompanysucks. This individual lost their job #bigbrothermonitorssocialmedia
- How about the brand burner who blunders into the weekly staff meeting five minutes late, moving chairs around, papers falling, muttering about traffic or his kid throwing up, then goes out of the room *again* to get a cup of coffee
- Then there's the brand burner, who one month into the job replies YES for her family of four to come to the small company Christmas party on a Saturday night, hosted by the boss with dinner purchased per person ahead of time. At party time, she and her family are no shows. No apology text the day of the party to her supervisor or to the party host, nor any real explanation or apology in the days after.

Or do you want to be:

- The employee who consistently is willing to develop the first draft of any document knowing that the first draft always receives the largest dose of criticism (especially from those who couldn't write a complete sentence if their life depended on it).
- The person who is so responsive to cell phone calls or emails at all hours of the night and day regardless of what global time zone he is in that he prompts a series of urban myths/jokes from his team about him answering the phone during the middle of a funeral service or a wedding or a medical procedure.
- The guy who *had* to be at a client meeting. He rolls his car on the way to the airport, but instead of missing his flight, he leaves his car in the ditch, hitchhikes to the airport, makes the flight, and wins the businesses. That was definitely a brand-building moment.
- The professional employee who volunteers to work with the marketing team and stays through a Friday and Saturday night, including standing at a copy machine for hours to print chunks of the document, to make sure that the document can be delivered on Monday.
- Then there's the brand builder who arrives at the conference room five minutes before a meeting (any meeting) is supposed to start, gets settled in with coffee or water or whatever, chats with peers about their weekend or perhaps has a little casual chit-chat with the boss prior to the meeting start, and then is totally focused on the matters at hand once the meeting officially starts.

When you come face-to-face with a decision that you think will impact your career, you may be making tradeoffs between impacts to your career and impacts to your family or personal life. We can't tell you what to do. We can tell you that we've made what we thought were "pro-career" decisions that, in the end, had no consequential impact on our careers but had a negative impact on our personal life. (There is only one kindergarten Holiday pageant that your child will be in and no digital reproduction of said pageant can make up for you missing it to attend a client meeting that could have been changed.)

Some of those decisions did have a positive impact on our careers in the long run. Both of us built strong relationships with clients as well as developing a reputation for "delivering." We also have made a few "pro-personal life" decisions for which, even though they may have kept us from getting to the top level in an organization, we have no regrets.

You will have a different suite of choices for which you will make the career/personal life tradeoffs.

YOU will make these.

You can seek advice from your mentor. You can ask friends. You can discuss this with your wife. You can ask your religious advisor.

The sad and sometimes frustrating reality about getting "help" with your decisions is that each of the individuals you talk to will tend to be limited by their own (sometimes narrow) life experiences and their advice can be skewed by their own fears, biases, selfish interests, and/or rationalizations of their own bold or cautious decisions they made along the way that may or may not have worked out well. That doesn't mean you shouldn't talk to people. You should.

Just know that in the end the decision is yours and no one really knows you as well as you or really cares about you as much as you do. (When David asked his mentor about moving to Colorado and the mentor said, "bad idea," David moved anyway. He has no idea how things would have turned out if he had not moved, and that's okay.)

The bottom line is pretty straight forward: you will make your decisions and you will be responsible for the outcomes of those decisions. So this simple question—are you a brand burner or a brand builder—can act as a touchstone when you're faced with those inevitable decisions that will impact your overall career

There's no right answer, either, but by simply taking a step back and looking at how your actions are going to be perceived by others can only help you in the long run.

MANAGE YOURSELF

Hey good job. Figuring out who you are is no walk in the park for most people. It's the reason that lots of people prefer to live in their own imaginary world. (Ever been to Comic-Con or a Raider's game?) Once you understand who you are, you need to figure out how that might work in the corporate world. This is the real beginning of the intersection between You and Them; it's where you start to figure out what "us" means. So, as you may have surmised, we've got some ideas to help you know how to apply your real You to the daily grind of the work place.

You are the CEO, COO, CIO, CPO and Big Bad Boss of *you* and *your career*. It's a great gig that no one else wants. That's right, no one wants to be responsible for your career. If someone tells you that they want that responsibility, we think you need to wonder why because "they" aren't "you." Only you can be you and only you can fully undertake and do everything that you can possibly do to achieve the things you want to achieve in your career. There's a lot of "you's" in that sentence. Let's take a look at some of things that President *YOU* should be thinking about and doing.

LEVERAGE YOUR ENERGY CYCLES

• • • • •

"Success is almost totally dependent upon drive and persistence. The extra energy required to make another effort or try another approach is the secret of winning."

—DENIS WAITLEY

"It's early in the morning now as I write this chapter. The house is quiet. I've had my first cup of coffee. I'm ready to crank. There is a reason I have selected this time to write. Writing is hard work and I know that it takes all of my brain power to write efficiently and effectively. I've learned over many years in the corporate world that I am most effective in the early mornings, and my brain is as ready now as it ever will be today to take on tough tasks. At this time of day, I know I can probably write the same amount in one hour that might take me two hours in the late afternoon or evening."

Simon is very clear about when he is most effective. Simon is an early bird who works best in the morning. Everyone is different in this way. Simon's wife is the opposite. She'll do her best writing late in the evening when the "muse" hits her, and she'll go into a zone for several hours without really noticing the time. Opposites attract!! The point here is to know yourself and how you work best. It's also really helpful to know your teammates and your boss so you can all work as effectively as possible together.

"I remember how liberating it was for me to finally be the one 'in charge,' who could decide when the weekly staff meetings would happen, or when our project teams would plan major brainstorming or strategy sessions," Simon says, "I could now schedule these around the high or low productivity zones for me and other key staff. Routine staff meetings could now happen at times of day (mid-afternoon for me) when my energy levels were on the fade for the day but my brain wasn't quite dead yet. Brainstorming sessions were always set for the mornings when I knew that I and my key team members would be at our best.

"The same goes for email. I have learned to dedicate certain zones in the day to the routine email monitoring and management. This is low energy stuff that I don't want to be carving into my precious zones of time when I can be highly productive. If something pops up in the email that takes a lot of brain power to deal with, I try to schedule it for a time in the day when I know I can kill it. This way, I am in control of my time, and I am handling the important issues to the best of my ability. Otherwise, it will take up way too much of my time when I was not planning on it. I'll do a poor job handling it, and the whole experience will frustrate me.

The point is simple. Know when you have your peak productivity times. This concept extends far beyond the daily or hourly energy cycles that we all experience. Over the course of each year, there are also cycles of time when you are more able to fully commit your time and energy to your job. Think of your productivity and commitment to your job during the weeks when you have close friends or relatives in town, one of your kids has a major sports tournament going on, or you have a newborn baby. Let's face it—you are in "survive" mode at work during these times. You are just trying to keep your head above water, not let any major balls drop, and make it through the day. This is nothing to be ashamed of. It's just part of the reality of life.

Now compare your productivity during these to the weeks to your productivity yield when you have nothing special on the calendar, or you are travelling on business with no family commitments in the evening. This is when you can be in "thrive" mode. You can spontaneously work late or on the weekend to do that extra special great job on the assignments at hand. You can initiate brainstorming sessions or new initiatives that can change the direction of your business. These are the times when you need to make up for those other weeks when you were distracted and put in the time and energy to blow the socks off your boss or the competition.

The best thing you can do during the down times is to take vacation days. This may not always be possible, but if it is, do it. The more people see you in "survive" mode as opposed to "thrive" mode, the more your personal brand is impacted. If you can't actually be gone from the office, communicate with your boss or your key staff what is going on in your life. There is nothing wrong with being a human being and having outside drains on your time and energy. This is better than people thinking that you just don't care about your job anymore.

Over the course of our careers, we have been amazed at how much mileage we have gotten out of a few key energy bursts of high productivity and "going that extra mile" when the opportunity was right for us. Once you earn your brand inside the company as the person that did this extra special great thing one time, that brand can live for a long time and last throughout several "down" energy cycles for months to come. That isn't to say that you rest on your laurels for six months every time you put in a little extra work on the weekend. Just recognize that these bursts of energy have the potential to yield lots of fruit and will often more than pay for themselves in terms of the recognition and rewards that follow.

The key is to be self-aware. You will have daily energy cycles—know these and leverage them to your advantage when you can. You will have weekly, monthly, and maybe even yearly cycles when you will have more energy or less energy to commit to true excellence on your job. Be aware of these as they are happening. Survive the downtimes and communicate your needs for time and space to your boss and team, and plan to leverage your high energy and productivity zones to the hilt to maximize your impact on the company and your personal brand.

SMILE

• • • • •

War is a game that is played with a smile.
If you can't smile, grin. If you can't grin,
keep out of the way till you can.

—WINSTON CHURCHILL

This one is very basic. Chances are you learned this long ago and it has helped you in every step of your career. But the importance of this makes it worth a refresher for you, and I guarantee you will remember this the next time a fuse is about to blow when someone—a colleague, a customer, a boss—does something so absolutely insane you can't believe it. When you are in those situations, start with a smile—but not a smirk.

This is about bringing positive energy to your efforts. Your grandparents called this a "can do" attitude and this is the same attitude that led to some of the greatest and most useful inventions of the twentieth century, including Velcro and the internet. Staying positive will rub off on your team and give them energy as they grind through the dog days of your project.

You know the person who maintains a receptive, positive attitude at all times (okay at nearly all times). That person drives you nuts. But secretly, you want to be that person. You want to be the one in the room that your boss looks to for support when he or she is looking for volunteers, making a joke, discussing a sensitive topic, or sharing disappointing news. If you haven't noticed already, there are enough sourpusses, naysayers, curmudgeons, and nervous nellies in the world, let alone in your company or in your working group. You don't need to be one of them. Rather, be the light and levity in the room, not the gloom and doom. There is a positive side to everything and showing a little humor, a willingness to take risks, and having a little fun goes a long way.

There are lots of other smaller examples of where simple smiling and cordial chit chat makes a difference. Think of all the little hallway exchanges you have every day, like walking by colleagues or total strangers as you are heading to a meeting or to the copy room. How hard is it to say hello, smile, and perhaps even make a pleasant comment such as "nice tie" or "thanks for your hard work"? People love to get noticed and love the attention. It always amazes us how self-important and serious people can be as they bluster their way around the office looking too busy to look you in the eye or say hello as they pass by. Does that impress you? Take a moment to think about how you act when you see people in the hallway, copy room, elevator, or wherever. Do you offer up a smile at least? Give it a try.

HANDLE YOUR OWN STUFF

• • • • •

"Those who enjoy responsibility usually get it; those who merely like exercising authority usually lose it."
—MALCOLM FORBES

When you start work, you will have to have conversations and deliver tough messages to people within your organization and to clients. It's something that you, no matter what position you hold, must do. It's not easy.

In Middle School, you probably asked someone to tell someone else that "you liked them." This use of the "romance intermediary" saved you the embarrassment of a negative response. While this methodology certainly has benefits for the social activities of a middle schooler, it is flat out gutless for adults of any age. Gutless and worthless. Middle school diplomacy does not work in the working world.

People will offer to help you all the time. When a peer says, "Do you want me to tell your boss that you deserve a promotion?" or "I'm going to have lunch with the CFO, and I'm going to tell her what a great job you did on the quarterly report," we have found that the best response is, "No, please don't do this. I will handle this myself." And then, *go* handle it.

Having a problem with a colleague? Don't ask someone else to fix it. *Fix it yourself.*

A subordinate is not doing their job well? Don't send a message through one of their peers. *Tell them yourself.* Now you may ask HR to go along with you when you confront a subordinate about subpar work, but you handle your own stuff when it comes to your career, your team, and your chunk of your business.

This doesn't mean that you don't delegate stuff. It means that you don't delegate the most delicate interpersonal communications that you, as a team leader, mid-manager, aspiring executive (whatever position you're holding) should be doing *yourself.*

You do this because it's the right thing to do, and it's quite honestly a sign of weakness to have others carry your water for you. You also do this to make sure that accurate, clear messages get presented to the individuals who need to hear them.

We know that this is not always the norm. We have observed senior executives send HR people to layoff high level staff. In fact, one HR person that we worked with was known as the "Angel of Death." When this person appeared in an office, it was frequently to lay someone off. A high-level executive in a branch office once saw her come into the office, and thinking that he may be the target for this HR grim reaper, he immediately grabbed his cell phone and ran off to the men's room where he reposed for several hours hoping that the angel would grow weary of waiting for him and leave. (Turns out he was not the target that day—his time would come about a year later.) The senior executive who should have been doing this himself simply didn't have the guts and thus turned the duties over to this poor HR person.

When you do screw up the courage to have a tough conversation with your boss, your peer, and eventually your subordinates, please think about what you are saying and the clarity of your message. Many people, both of us included, tend to use "watered-down" language when delivering an uncomfortable message. A colleague (a senior consultant) in one of our regional offices was struggling. His clients didn't have enough work for him, and other offices were not engaging him to support their clients. He was in a weird place in his life and career and was just meeting basic performance expectations for someone at his level. This came up during the course of a meeting on another topic that was attended by this individual's boss, the regional manager, and an Executive Vice President (EVP). They discussed how they might light a fire under this senior individual and get him pointed in the right direction. The individual's boss, who really needed to handle this, deferred to the EVP. The problem was that the EVP in question was known for the passive voice. He was rarely direct on difficult issues— NEVER. Off the EVP went to have a long lunch with the underperforming senior consultant. He got back to the individual's boss and regional manager and told them that the problem was solved. "I told him that I couldn't say that I wouldn't be unhappy if he didn't consider not doing that," the EVP told the regional manager. The senior consultant couldn't decipher the instructions hidden in the amazing quadruple negative sentence and ended up leaving the company a short time later.

Have you ever played the game "telephone" with a large group of people? It's amazing how a simple message can be changed as it passes from person to person. Some in your company will use this to their advantage. They will carry messages from one person to the next and modify these messages to suit their particular needs. We have seen senior executives get "played" by a subordinate who twists the messages that they carry between these individuals. Only when the senior executives communicate directly with each other do they realize that they are actually "on the same page" and that they were being played by this individual. We believe the term of art for this is "getting clowned."

When you let others carry your messages, they get diluted, reconstituted, changed, and mangled. Just handle your own stuff. Oh and try to avoid quadruple negatives.

INVEST IN YOUR NETWORKS

• • • • •

"Business is not just doing deals; business is having great products, doing great engineering, and providing tremendous service to customers. Finally, business is a cobweb of human relationships."

—ROSS PEROT

It will not be breaking news to you that relationships have always played a critical role in business success. You also may have noticed that one of the things that separates the high flyers of the business world from the rest of the pack is their ability to draw on vast networks of business and personal contacts to develop new business or perform their business functions more efficiently and effectively. But you don't need to be a high flyer (yet) to have your own networks of relationships, and it is never too early to start building and maintaining your network. These networks are not built overnight. They are not built by accident and they need attention to grow and stay valuable over time.

With the onset of social media tools such as Facebook and LinkedIn, it is now easier than ever to build your network and access your contacts in various ways. Your network can now easily extend far beyond the walls of your company, and this network can become part of your own personal brand. Individual networks are fast becoming measuring sticks for people's value in the marketplace. Ask any recruiter—a company employee that is highly networked across their industry carries a higher value than one that has merely kept their head down and done their job without ever building a network of relationships outside the company.

What about you? As you step onto the first rungs of the proverbial career ladder, think consciously about your various networks of relationships. Are you investing appropriately in these various networks to nurture and grow the relationships you have and make your networks bigger and stronger? Take a moment now to write down a few lists of some of the major networks in your life. This could include your external professional networks (outside of your company) such as clients, competitors, vendors, industry associations, recruiters and former employees. Now, how about your more social networks of friends, neighbors, local business relationships, members of your church or club or other social organizations.

Then consider the internal professional relationships inside your company, including working groups, peers, senior managers, technical staff and support staff. Chances are that when you stop and think about it, your networks are bigger than you think. Now the question is, how strong are these networks, and are you investing in these and/or using them effectively?

For each of the people in the external networks you listed, consider asking yourself a few questions:

- Do you know what each of these people does for a living?
- Do you know what types of clients they serve or what types of new business they would like to have?
- Do they all know what you do for a living?
- Do they know what types of clients you serve or what type of new business you would like to have?

For the people inside your company, consider asking yourself these questions:

- Do you know anything about their life outside of work?
- Do you know anything about their goals or desired next opportunities within the company?
- Do they know anything about your life outside of work?
- Do they know anything about your goals or desired next opportunities within the company?

The point here is that the more you know about the people in your network and the more they know about you, then the more you will be able to help each other go where you each want to go. How would your friend at church ever refer a potential client to you if they don't know what you do or what types of clients you would be seeking? How can you ever help your neighbor's son find a job in your industry if you don't know the son or don't know anyone else in your industry? What goes around comes around, and the more you find opportunities to help people across your network, then the stronger these networks and relationships become and the more you will benefit from them in return.

It is also a fact that more and more customers are shopping for products and services by tapping into social networks to find who and what other people they know tend to like. More and more companies are recruiting for positions using social networks to find highly networked people who already have good jobs in the hopes that they might be interested in a better job.

You will never know exactly what benefits will come your way as a result of the investments you make now to build and nurture your networks. But make no mistake that these networks will pay off. So, take the time to join the social network revolution, set goals for yourself to grow and invest in your networks; let people know what you do and what you are interested in, and look for opportunities to help people whenever you can.

HOW TO HANDLE CRITICISM

• • • • •

"Criticism may not be agreeable, but it is necessary. It fulfils the same function as pain in the human body. It calls attention to an unhealthy state of things."

—WINSTON CHURCHILL

In case you haven't figured it out by now, we have some shocking news for you: you're not perfect! You never were and you never will be. That sounds harsh, but don't worry, your mother still loves you and probably a few other people do, too. And the good news is that they don't expect you to be perfect, and neither do your colleagues and supervisors at work.

What does this mean to you? It means you will do things imperfectly. And people will notice. And they will tell you. It's called criticism, and it happens—to everyone. Everything is going to be okay as long you know to expect it along the way, and you do your best to not make a jackass out of yourself when it hits you in the face.

As luck would have it, the chances are that your imperfection may well extend to your (in)ability to accept criticism in a professional manner. If that is the case, you will not be alone. Accepting criticism is hard, and most people have to learn this skill over time along with the many other overt and covert skills necessary for survival in the workplace.

So now, instead of getting a fairly decent B+ when you perform moderately well and get over ten things out of a hundred wrong—allowing you to still please your parents adequately to get them to still help with your tuition check next semester—instead, you might get some angry red ink on your draft client presentation and have to face a slightly frustrated and impatient supervisor that doesn't think you are hot stuff after all. Are you ready for this? You can be.

While it was over twenty-five years ago now, Simon can remember clear as day a not-so-proud moment in his early working career when he was not prepared for criticism. He was fairly fresh out of a top graduate school, feeling pretty self-satisfied as the bright-eyed eager associate engineer at his new company, when a Supervising Engineer asked him for assistance with a client presentation she was to give the following week. Simon's PowerPoint skills were adequate, and he thought he understood the material. He had never delivered or written or even witnessed such a client presentation, but of course this was going to be a slam dunk. Yet another opportunity to shine and impress his new company with his creativity and sales skills!

Not so much. Picture the arrow that not just misses the target but somehow leaves the arena and maims some innocent child selling lemonade across the street. Simon can still picture the small, neatly organized office, sitting across from the Supervisor with the glare of the California sun backlighting her and no doubt exposing his red face and the tears continuously welling up in his eyes as he tried to wipe them before they streamed down his face and compounded his embarrassment. She was walking through the presentation—now riddled with page after page of red ink—highlighting the profound incompetence that was a "perfect" presentation.

Ouch. Simon could not get back to his desk fast enough to not only compose himself, but start working on a major re-write that would better hit the mark. He doesn't remember too many details after that moment, which is probably a good thing. The trauma was over. He survived, and he must have made big strides towards a more presentable product. It is interesting to note that Simon went on to have a great working relationship with this Supervisor for years after, even developing a close a friendship that continues to this day. She made him better at his job that day and continued to do so through many future less-traumatic feedback sessions in the years that followed.

Now, could she have been more gentle with her feedback? Of course, but engineers are not always known for their empathy, and that is not really the point here. The point is, Simon was not yet performing at the level that his company needed him to be for the ongoing development of efficient, effective, high-quality work products. And while his supervisor might have gotten a little enjoyment out of taking Simon down a notch, he would be the first to admit he probably deserved it and it was probably the tough love he needed to raise his game to where it needed to be. In the end, he was fortunate that someone told it to him straight rather than delaying his growth by avoiding the conflict that comes with direct and honest feedback.

This story highlights a trite but true statement. Constructive criticism is truly a gift. The sooner you recognize this and identify these precious nuggets of criticism for the gift that they are, the better you will be able to receive these gifts and the more you will benefit from them. Many supervisors are not courageous enough to offer honest, constructive feedback. They shy away from conflict and assume someone else will deliver the feedback to that employee someday. By avoiding these hard conversations, they are unwittingly doing a disservice to the employee, their company, and possibly themselves if that employee does not grow as quickly to benefit the company.

In his current role as a small business owner, Simon has worked hard to improve on his own ability to provide direct, honest feedback to employees and have the hard conversations to hold his staff accountable in a firm but constructive manner. This is harder than it looks, and it's a weakness that he struggled to overcome on a consistent basis.

One thing that helped his progress in this area was the good fortune of working with a truly unique staff member named Heather that has proven to be the best example of how to properly receive constructive criticism he has ever met. Sometimes our teachers come in unexpected forms: Picture a street-wise, Chicago-born, former waitress and softball player with little to no corporate experience and sub-par computer skills. Combine this with the ability to talk her way out of any traffic ticket or charm the most hostile customer, and add an incredible team spirit and passion for success, and you have Heather.

Now, like all of us, and like everyone in Simon's company, including Simon, Heather makes mistakes. Simon has observed her behavior pattern after making these mistakes—which would be familiar to anyone that knows her. Her first reaction when told of these mistakes is usually a still-not-quite-polished, "Oh $%&^!" and then, "I'm sorry, I'm sorry, I'm sorry," and then, "What do we need to do," and then after that, they form a game plan for recovery and next steps. Then, finally, "Thank you. Thank you for helping me. I will get better. I will not make this mistake again. Thank you!" There is no defensiveness. There is no passing the buck. There is immediate recognition that there is an issue to solve that is her responsibility and she will work hard to not make this kind of mistake again. That is all Simon needs to hear as her boss. Both can move on with their day. Nothing personal. No tears. Just business.

So, you too will find yourself criticized in your early working years. And you will most likely find that there is so much to learn in any new job that you will inevitably make mistakes and the criticism will come. Some of this criticism may be a bit unjustified and perhaps even a bit malicious. But much of it may well be deserved and there will almost always be nuggets of truth in there and gifts of improvement potential for you to unwrap. (Go ahead and join us singing the Kelly Clarkson "What doesn't kill you makes you stronger" tune here ... .) So be prepared. And be grateful, as hard as that will seem at first.

And for the CliffsNotes readers in the room (a dated term, we know—you can Google it), a few practical survival tips for those early criticism encounters:

- Breathe, calm your heartbeat, go into Zen mode—you are now The Listener, not the Talker.
- Resist the temptation to defend yourself immediately—let them talk and finish saying what they have to say before you jump in.
- Seek to truly understand—ask clarifying questions, take notes. Treat this as a valuable opportunity and get the most out of this you possibly can. Keep repeating to yourself: this is a gift, this is a gift.
- Be the grownup in the room—thank them for their input, accept responsibility, and promise to work to improve in the future. If there is a glaring mistake and misunderstanding you can of course try to communicate your understanding of the situation, but it should not sound defensive, and it should not take away from your ownership of the issue and your willingness to improve moving forward.
- Work very hard to not repeat the error. Once you have a moment to yourself, write down your key takeaways from the episode and how you will behave differently in the future. If there are still any questions in your mind as to what you did wrong and or what you should do differently moving forward, get those questions answered sooner rather than later so you can avoid the same mistake in the future.

BALANCING YOUR AMBITION
WITH PATIENCE

· · · · ·

"Every man is said to have his peculiar ambition.
Whether it be true or not, I can say for one
that I have no other so great as that of being
truly esteemed of my fellow men,
by rendering myself worthy of their esteem."

—ABRAHAM LINCOLN

As you may have discovered by now, succeeding in a corporate environment involves a lot of balancing acts. One balancing act that we have personally struggled with over the years has been between ambition and patience. That is, when is it best for you to bide your time and let things play out, and when is it best for you to push hard for that next opportunity, higher salary, or position of greater responsibility?

In an ideal world, employees would receive the next opportunity or assignment exactly when they are ready for it, and the best people would be first in line to get the best assignments, and the next promotions. Sorry if this is news to you, but life doesn't work that way either inside or outside of corporate America.

The squeaky wheel gets the grease, as the old saying goes, and the person who is best connected, rather than best qualified, might be the one that is next in line for the raise or promotion. Sometimes, though, the squeaky wheel gets annoying and gets fired, so this isn't always the best course of action either. Like many balancing acts in the work place, there is no single right or wrong answer to this, and you need to understand the landscape where you're operating, and play the course accordingly.

There are certainly times when you need to temper your ambition and exercise patience. One example of this is during tough economic times when the company's growth is static or shrinking and there are no real positions available for you to grow into and no extra money floating around to handout big raises or bonuses. You need to be conscious of the big picture for your company, your division, and your boss so that your attitude and ambitions do not come off as disconnected from the atmosphere of the company. Rather, you need to show an awareness of the company situation and perhaps offer some new ideas as to how you can contribute in a greater capacity—maybe without immediate reward for these extra efforts but with the understanding that you will get recognized eventually for these additional contributions.

Simon had one employee that worked for him for many years who was of the school of thought that if you ask for a raise and/or a promotion every month (regardless of company financials or their actual performance), you will eventually wear your boss down and get what you are asking for sooner than you otherwise would. While this may be true in some cases, this approach also carries a real risk of annoying your boss, who would rather not have these high-maintenance, never-satisfied employees on his or her team. Bosses are people too. They like to be appreciated and thanked for whatever bonuses or promotions they are authorized to hand out, and not always treated like they should have done more and are holding back from giving you something you deserve.

There are also times when you need to exercise your ambition to the maximum. It's okay to capitalize on positive events in the workplace and your own personal successes and contributions to the company bottom line. If you have just landed the biggest account the company has ever known, or if your division outperformed the rest for the second year in a row, you need to be compensated in a significant manner that will incentivize you to continue to deliver this kind of performance in the future. If you meet resistance to these demands and find that you are not receiving the kind of compensation or recognition that can keep you motivated, then you need to recognize that the story you are telling inside your company (that is landing on deaf ears) might be quite convincing to a competitor that will be willing to pay you your real value in the marketplace. You need to be brave enough to explore these avenues in order to satisfy your ambitious side and know that you are getting compensated at true fair market value. You deserve no less.

Looking back at our own careers, David thinks he probably erred on the side of being a bit too patient and easy on his bosses, a bit too reluctant to explore his value in the marketplace, and possibly not being demanding enough to get what he perceived to be fair compensation for his value in the marketplace. So, in the spirit of "Do as I say, not as I do" maybe you could try to err on the more aggressive side of things—push a bit more often than you are comfortable to get that next assignment, raise, or promotion, and don't be afraid to talk to headhunters and other companies to test your fair market value. This is an area where your mentors and your network can really help you to understand your value in the marketplace and understand when and how best to make your value and ambitions widely known to those who might be able to recognize and reward you.

Find Mentors

• • • • •

"Wise men don't need advice. Fools won't take it."
—Benjamin Franklin

This is a topic that really could fit into several different chapters of this book. We put it here because mentors are the people who can help you get positively noticed. A good mentor will tell you when the stuff you are doing is getting you negatively noticed and can move you in a positive direction. They can help you with your self-awareness. They can help you practice and prepare. They can help you deliver successful work products, and when the time comes, they can help you lead.

Mentoring is a part of every element of climbing the ladder. That being said—let's talk about what it means for you.

If you really want to know who you are, and what areas of your business and personal skill sets require your attention, then a mentor is a great place to start. David has often said that finding a mentor was never something he put a lot of thought into until late in his career. "I looked around and realized that I didn't really have one. I was always pretty used to carving my own path and letting my own achievements speak for themselves. Whatever I accomplished, I did on my own and there was a certain pride and self-sufficiency that comes with that. Hooray for me. What I did not realize however, is that doing it 'on my own' would only take me so far.

"It was at this fairly late stage in my career when I had my 'a-ha' moment about mentors. I started to see people younger than me leap a few rungs at a time on the corporate ladder. They were talented, sure, but it was clear they were benefiting immensely from strong mentor relationships with senior staff around the company. I couldn't tell whether or not they had consciously or unconsciously created these relationships, but I could see that it mattered. They were getting places in two years that took others ten. It's not a stretch to say that in many cases these benefits were quite disproportional to their not-so-unique talents and abilities. What separated them from the pack? Why did they get the job when others didn't? In many cases, there was not a lot else to point to except mentors."

"Don't get me wrong. I don't begrudge their success. I point this out to say that you don't need to make the same mistakes I did by ignoring this critical aspect of the business game. Mentors matter. And if you don't have one now, you need one. If you only have one, you should probably find two more. I don't care who you are, or where you are in your career. There are always next steps, and mentors can get you up those steps just like the Six Million Dollar Man—better, stronger, and faster. This may sound a bit calculating, but this is the reality of getting ahead. Now you know."

What does it mean to have mentors? These are people inside and outside of your company that typically are senior to you, that have a few more battle scars than you, that you respect, and that are willing to give you a bit of their time to think about you and help advise you as you navigate your career. In the best of circumstances, these might be people that are rising stars themselves. Then as they rise, they bring you along with them and you help each other become successful. Or they are well networked in the company, and they can help you get noticed by that VP that has just started looking for a trusted deputy for a critical assignment.

More often than not, though, effective mentors are merely trusted advisors for you who operate outside your direct reporting lines. These are people that are not immersed in the day to day politics of your situation—they can see the forest above the trees and offer you some welcome perspective on your situation.

Good mentors don't solve your problems for you (don't expect them too), but rather they coach you to success over the long term. Good mentors don't pull punches—they tell it like it is, and it is up to you to have thick skin, listen well, and act appropriately on their advice. It may take years for a mentor/ protégé relationship to mature and yield fruit. You never know when or how these relationships are going to help you, but believe me, they will help.

Ideally, you will want to have several mentors at the same time, and these mentors will come and go over the years. As you reach different levels in your career, you may need different types of mentors to help you overcome certain challenges or weaknesses in your own thinking or skill sets. This is not school anymore. You don't have to do all your homework on your own. You are allowed to get help, and in fact, you will need it.

One thing to be mindful of is that mentors are human too. They are not always right, and they have only as much wisdom as their own individual experiences have allowed them. This is why it's good to have several mentors rather than one. You can benefit from multiple people's experience and integrate the advice from multiple perspectives.

Another thing that took us a long time to realize about mentors: they like it! People are often shy about finding mentors and procrastinate seeking anyone out to ask for help. You will find that when you start seeking people out, most mentors worth their salt are flattered to be asked and tend to enjoy the role. I know in the many cases when one of us has been a mentor to others, either formally or informally, we always find it as a welcome break from our usual work day to spend a bit of time thinking about other people's issues and problems. It can be very fun and satisfying to help make an impact on someone else's career without a lot of time or trouble.

Now as you contemplate finding and asking someone to be your mentor, you don't have to get all formal about it. Just as you don't ask a boy or girl to go steady the first moment you meet them, you don't need to open the first conversation with "will you be my mentor?" See how they react when you knock on their door and say, "Hey do you have a few minutes to help me with something?" If you get a positive reaction and a few minutes of their time, then they are likely the type that might be receptive to this role.

You could even end the first or second conversation with a comment like: "This has been really helpful for me to discuss this with you, and I really appreciate your time. Would you mind if I occasionally come back to you every month or two to have brief discussions with you on topics such as this? I think it would really help my career." Now what are they going to say? No? You have just shown that you respect them, you respect their time, you find them full of wisdom, and you are asking for very little from them for huge value to you. Chances are you are well on your way to a good mentoring relationship.

As your mentoring relationship continues, don't forget that your mentor needs a little love too. Not a lot, but a little. This type of love comes in the form of actually following some if not all of their advice and reporting back to them on progress or outcomes. If they tell you to read a book, you should read it, and send them a short note thanking them for the tip and maybe noting a few things you got out of the book. If they tell you to go meet with someone, do it and send a short email thanking them and making it clear that you followed their advice. This shows respect for them and that they are not wasting their time talking to you.

Recognize When You Need a Change

· · · · ·

"To become different from what we are,
we must have some awareness of what we are."

—Eric Hoffer

There will come a time in your career that you will have to face the inevitable—change. Everyone who has worked in Corporate America has had to deal with needing to move on.

The first few times this happened to Simon, he didn't have enough experience and self-awareness to realize it, "If I had known what was going on, I probably wouldn't have wanted to share this finding with anyone else in my company for fear that they might think I was disloyal or not a long term employee worth investing in. Fortunately for me, I had some more experienced people around me that were able to recognize this need for me. They put enough variety in front of me that my thirst for change was satiated for the time being."

Our main point here is that everyone goes through phases in their career when the role they are in and the tasks at hand are no longer as exciting or inspiring as they once might have been. Those weekly staff meetings that you once looked forward to, prepared for diligently, and saw as opportunities for team building and process improvement have now become a bit mundane and inconvenient. Your own lack of passion—as much as you try to hide it—is probably rubbing off on others and you are no longer serving as the source of inspiration and passion that you were two years ago. While these phases can be tough to recognize and accept at first, particularly when you are experiencing this for the first time, they are quite normal and important to recognize, accept, and act upon accordingly.

So, let's assume you are able to recognize this feeling. Then what? The thought of going to your boss and telling him or her that your job no longer excites you is not always a fun prospect. Don't worry. This doesn't have to be your first course of action, and if you do get around to this eventually, it won't come as a big shock and it probably won't be the first time your boss has heard this.

Your first course of action is to start a process of introspection, self-awareness, and education. You need to understand what it is about your current situation that is no longer exciting you. Maybe there are parts that are still exciting and parts that are not. Has your situation around you changed for the worse somehow, or have your feelings simply changed about the same job and role that has always existed? Are there any obvious paths in the company that would likely be more interesting and exciting to you, where you think you could come to work with the same passion that you used to have for your current role? Understanding your current feelings and educating yourself about the potential opportunities around you is an excellent first step.

This is an excellent time to talk to your mentors as well. Your mentor can provide extremely useful perspective to help you understand your feelings and perhaps expand the horizons of your thinking about potential next steps and opportunities. Your mentor might know of jobs in the company that don't even exist right now, but he or she recognizes a void in the company's capabilities and therefore a job opportunity for someone—perhaps even you. This ability to "see around corners" is what mentors will bring to you.

One of Simon's favorite stories related to this type of mentor assistance came about five years into his career when he was going through the first of many "I need a change" phases. At this time, he had been living in Northern California for about seven years and felt the need to travel again and see the world a bit more. He didn't have enough experience to know that he should talk to people about his feelings, and had decided on his own that there were no available opportunities in the company for travel. He came across a couple opportunities that interested him—a White House fellowship and a position at the US Agency for International Development. There were some definite advantages: they would be something new. He would get to spend some more time in DC, where he had enjoyed living previously, and he actually might travel a bit (considered a positive in those early days!). The downside was obvious: the pay would be much lower than his current

44

role. The other thing these two opportunities had in common was they required several references, which meant he had to notify people at work of his plans in order to ask them for a reference. This is when the mentor network started to work for him without his even asking for it.

Before Simon knew it, a new job was created in the company to fill a void in the company's services that he didn't even know had existed. Among the people to whom he had gone to get a reference was a guy willing to be creative and look around a bit on his behalf. This local manager talked to some other VPs that had been experiencing a need for someone to work on behalf of some of the senior leaders in the company to track regulatory changes in our field and make presentations to clients and senior office managers around the country about what the regulatory changes might mean to our clients. This required regular travel back to DC for conferences and regular visits with senior company offices at corporate meetings around the country. Oh, and this new position that did not used to exist, happened to pay about 20 percent more than Simon's current role. And best of all, it was something new!

Now, this story may be a bit unusual since Simon didn't even recognize what was going on with his feelings, and he was fortunate to have made a positive impression with people that had the creativity and authority to look out for him and hand him a significant breakthrough in his career. This may seem like a lucky break, and of course it was to some extent. Looking back on this though, we would also argue that Simon did a lot of things right by simply recognizing that he needed a change before his work suffered and before his reputation in the company was damaged in any way. He talked to people around him to give the company an opportunity to make something happen for him rather than simply quitting. (Luckily, the reference requirement forced him to do this or he might not have taken this important step.) It is now no longer surprising that in the maybe twenty years since this story, a similar type of story has unfolded on nearly every occasion when Simon has needed a change (occurring like clock-work about every three to five years). Looking back, he now sees the course of his career as a series of tacks to the left and right, moving up parallel and intersecting ladders rather than a slow and steady climb up a single corporate ladder in a single direction. Knowing himself well enough to know when it was time to make a leap to another ladder allowed him to climb the ladders faster and enjoy the journey and the view a bit more along the way.

Who Are You—Last Looks

We've been talking a lot about You. It might be a bit much, even for "you." It's important that you figure out who you are and what you can do so you can survive and thrive as a part of "them." This voyage of discovery requires, as you have now discovered, a fair bit of introspection coupled with input from others who can provide honest feedback.

The importance of this cannot be overstated. An honest understanding of "you" is important in all areas of your life, not just the workplace. Knowing "you" is likely to be helpful at home, at the local pub, with your pinochle group, and in many other aspects of your life. It can be painful and awkward, but we hope you find it to be worthwhile.

It might also shine some light on what you are doing in your career. You want to understand who "you" are so you can figure out how to get the most out of this arranged marriage between "you" and "them," or if maybe "you" and "them" should part ways. We had a colleague who was promoted, and then promoted again within an eight-month time frame and then left the company four months later. He had discovered that he didn't like the pressure of being in a management role. He made a very mature decision about who he was and what he valued and moved to a job with another organization that had less pressure, less time commitment, and less pay. He understood who he was (the "you") and that helped him make a difficult career decision.

Time marches on and things change with time. Your personal circumstances are likely to change about as often as your favorite NBA superstar changes teams. Family size (kids, spouse, significant other, dogs, cats, llamas, etc.), favorite restaurant, music you listen to, easiest way to get to work, hairstyle, hair color, and whether or not you like to wear socks on the weekend are among the things in your life that will change over time. You will change and that is an immutable fact of life. Some things, like bad habits, are things you want to change and you can indeed change these things. But those aren't the real You.

The thing that is very likely to not change is the core You. This is the real "you." It's the most positive elements of you, your core. These are the things "you" are the best at doing; the things that give you the most pleasure in life. As David says, "My hair is shorter and it's turning (okay—it is) gray, but I still love music and sports and I get the most pleasure out of helping others. It's been that way for decades. This is the real me." That's him.

You, well, you gotta be "you."

TWO

You and the Boss

Get Noticed—Develop Your Brand

YOU ARE DEFINED BY YOU, BUT AS AN EMPLOYEE YOU WILL ALSO, IN part, be defined by Them. Them is a big term that refers to your boss(es), coworkers, customers, clients, the receptionist, shareholders, your team-mates on the company coed softball team, etc. They work with you, interact with you, possibly eat lunch with you, say good morning and good night to you, and size you up pretty quickly. It's just what people do.

For now, let's focus on your boss(es). You want Them—your bosses—to know the best You. You want your brand to be built on the solid core of who You are and what value you can bring every day when you walk through those big glass doors and say good morning to everyone. You need to take the elements of You that you have discovered and adapt these elements to your bosses. This is how you'll define and build your positive personal brand within the context of your business life.

For clarity, every one of Them is important. We live in a very small world (and we're truly sorry if those two words cause a never-ending loop of a song associated with a ride at Disneyland to be pounding through your head all day today). You need to take the long view. The guy in sales who plays right field on the softball team may not be very good at softball, but may someday be your boss or maybe even your customer. You will have created a brand with this person while playing softball or seeing him at the company cafeteria during lunch breaks. Keep that in your mind when you're tempted to yell at him because he's a lousy softball player.

YOU WANT TO GET NOTICED

• • • • •

"You wanna hot tip? Bet the jockey"
—BOB, AN USHER AT KEENELAND RACE TRACK,
LEXINGTON, KY

Interesting advice from a dude who looks like he doesn't win most of his bets. The concept is straightforward. Jockeys have a track record (horrible pun intended). They have a winning percentage, and if they win more often than they lose that would tell the betting public that, over the long haul, they are going to turn your bets into big bills (as in legal tender—the kinds of bills with Jacksons and Franklins on them) instead of torn up betting tickets.

Jockeys get noticed when they are winners. There is a way for you to get noticed as a "winner" in the business world. There are things you can do, behaviors you can exhibit, Instagram posts that you post, clothes you can wear, and things you can say that will get you noticed.

Please note that "notice" is an interesting term. People get noticed for the good things they do, but they also get noticed all the time for bad or inappropriate behavior. Go hang out in an airport and do some people watching. It's the unusual people doing the unusual things that catch your eye. They are dressed strangely, talking to themselves, carrying odd-shaped parcels, talking way too loudly, etc. They are being "noticed" and you are the one who is "noticing" them.

So what if you notice the crazy randos at the airport? There's nothing you can do about them, is there? No, not really. There is, however, a lesson to be learned from them. Crazy tends to stand out in a very bad way. That is NOT going to be you. Your doctrinal approach to "notice" is that you want to get noticed for the positive things you do, and you want to get noticed by the right people that can help you and your career. This takes a lot more effort than getting noticed for being crazy but it has a lot more benefit as well.

Positive notice requires positive actions and activities. It also requires that you be thoughtful, a little bit strategic, and willing to do things that you might otherwise prefer to not do. It takes more effort on your part for you to be noticed for positive reasons (than for negative reasons) and by the right people (who can help you—like your boss) so we'll give you some concepts that can help you get the positive notice you deserve. You want to be the jockey on whom everyone wants to place their bets.

KNOW YOUR BOSS

• • • • •

No man goes before his time—unless the boss leaves early.
—GROUCHO MARX

Think back to all of your teachers and professors you had while you were a student. Were they all the same? Did they expect or reward the same type of behavior from you? How about all of the bosses and supervisors you have had so far? Chances are that they all have had their individual quirks and peculiarities that took you a while to learn.

Once you finally learned the (usually unwritten) rules, life became a lot easier because you could anticipate the types of behavior that defined "success" in your teacher's mind, or at least the behavior that would keep you out of harm's way. This is a critical aspect of succeeding in any corporate environment. Just as learning what each of your teachers thought was important enabled you to prepare more effectively for your tests and get better grades in school, knowing your boss will enable you to survive and thrive in the work place.

You need to be a true student of your boss—knowing his or her daily routines, office behavior, working style, preferences, motivations, strengths, weaknesses, and goals. What makes her tick? Why did he take on this job, and what does he want to do next? Does he get to work early? Does she stay late? Does he mind being interrupted, or would he prefer that you schedule time to talk? What does she like to do during lunch? Does he like you to take actions on your own and ask for forgiveness later? Does she prefer that you consult her before taking any kind of action, big or small? How much involvement does he want in your daily or weekly affairs? Would she prefer that you keep her in the loop all the time, or just deliver the right numbers at the end of the month? Who does he tend to speak favorably about and why? You get the idea.

This isn't about being a spineless sycophant and only doing what your boss wants you to do all the time. This is about knowing the landscape in which you will be operating each day and acting accordingly. Golfers know this as "playing the course." You need to adjust your game for the particular golf course you are playing on. What might work on one course—wild drives that you can get away with since all the fairways are next to each other—might be way too risky on another course where the fairways are narrow and surrounded by water or thick brush.

This is about doing the easy stuff in the "right" way as defined by your current boss. If they like to see an agenda twenty-four hours before every meeting, then you need to learn this and then act accordingly. Even though your last boss may have been okay with getting the agenda out an hour before the meeting, it's not okay now. Don't fight this even if you think this is too demanding. You have to develop the agenda anyway, so it's no additional work for you to meet this schedule.

David had a new boss one time that insisted on reviewing every document that was going to go out the door to any client. He needed it twenty-four hours ahead of time, and it needed to be double spaced so he could mark it up more easily. Did this annoy David a bit? Yes! "I had been sending out documents to clients for ten years on my own without anyone reviewing them, and I had my own personal pride in my writing and my attention to detail. I would've never sent out anything that wasn't great. Plus, I hated printing everything double spaced—it was a waste of my time and a waste of paper. But was I going to fight this? No way. It was going to get me nowhere except in the doghouse with my new boss."

So David developed a better strategy to handle the problem. He flooded his boss with as many documents to review as he could, making sure the documents were as impeccable as possible, in the hopes that the boss would appreciate his productivity, and David could earn his trust so that the boss didn't need to review everything. David eventually did earn this trust, but for about six months, David also received some extremely helpful writing tips as well as excellent coaching on certain strategic approaches to take with our clients. "It was a win-win, and I was relieved that I did not fight the new rules."

It took us both a while in our careers to realize that our bosses tended to always view their current position as a stepping stone to the next position. While this is certainly not always the case, you will probably see this a majority of the time in your career too. What does this mean? For one thing, it means that your boss may be more interested in short-term gains and "polishing the numbers" for this year's or next year's books rather than significant investments in time and resources this year that might make the short term numbers look poor but have a long-term positive impact on the company. It is similar to the hesitation and reluctance that we see with our politicians and city officials who don't want to raise taxes or spend a lot of money this year since they will be up for re-election next year, even when they know it is in the best long-term interest of their jurisdiction.

The fact that your boss has his or her eyes on the next promotion also means there are various things they are trying to accomplish or people they are trying to impress to get to that next level. You need to be aware of these things and these people too. This is where you can help. It will be a win-win for you and your boss if you can do whatever you can to help your boss get where he or she is trying to go. You can probably guess what these things are, but you may not need to guess. Just ask. It doesn't need to be the first question you ask your boss, but at some point when you are away from the office—maybe on a car ride or over dinner on a business trip—ask about his or her motivations and goals then ask what you can do to help with these. There is very little risk in doing this and potentially a huge upside for you. It shows that you think about other people other than yourself and you can be a loyal partner in your boss's quest for success.

Know Your Boss's Goals

At one of the companies David and Simon both worked for, every senior manager had their "10K" goals. These were a customized set of annual goals—usually no more than five or six—that determined the annual bonuses for these senior managers. The "10K" referred to the ten thousand possible points that could be earned by each manager. The points were allocated among the various goals, and they were weighted to incentivize certain behaviors that were deemed important to that individual's contribution to the company's overall success that year. The goals were both vague, subjective goals such as "collaborate well with other divisions in the company" and specific, quantifiable goals such as "achieve X percent gross margin." You can imagine the shameless scrambling that used to take place in the final quarter of each year as these senior managers would be trying to complete their goals and fill up their 10K bingo cards with all the "right" meetings and collaboration sessions to position themselves for their bonus. All of a sudden around October of each year, senior managers that you had never spoken to all year were buddying up to you and asking if you could wring a couple more percentage points of margin out of your client in the fourth quarter.

While humorous in many respects, it also highlights the fact that these bosses are people too. They have their own bosses to impress and their own families to feed. It also highlights the very real opportunity that exists for the middle managers and staff that were the next level down from this 10K group to learn and help them achieve their boss's 10K goals. If you can make a major contribution to your boss earning their bonus, chances are that good things will flow your way as well.

Simon started asking to see his boss's 10K goals early in the year, so he could better understand the landscape and better help his boss "play the course" that year. "With these goals in mind, I could make it easier for my boss and colleagues all year long—inviting them to meetings where they would meet the right clients or creating opportunities for collaboration with other groups." While this may seem a bit transparent and shameless in its own respect, it really was just extending and accelerating the behavior that the CEO was trying to incentivize that year. It had an added benefit of aligning Simon's behavior with that of the senior managers.

It can never hurt to be armed with a bit more knowledge of who is trying to do what each year, and it might surprise you how much you can help contribute to the cause and position yourself for recognition and reward along the way.

BE PART OF THE SOLUTION

• • • • •

"God grant me the serenity to accept the things I cannot change, the courage to change the things I can, and the wisdom to know the difference."
—REINHOLD NIEBUHR

Companies are dynamic. Just like an amoeba which is constantly changing its shape, companies and organizations change stuff. The key word here is change, and they change because they can. A new executive ascends to the throne and decides what the predecessor was doing needs to be changed. They then proceed to change things.

That should never be a surprise to the working masses. It might be an organizational change, it might be a business process change, it might be a software change or a hardware change, it might be a change in your benefits. We can guarantee that you will not always like the change, but if you want to get noticed by your boss, you'll need to figure out how to embrace these changes and help move the company forward.

We've worked long enough in the corporate arena that we've seen companies go from A to B and back to A again.

We remember when it was all the rage to combine vacation and sick leave into one big bucket and call it Personal Time Off. Twenty years later, the next "big thing" was this great idea to give you one bucket for sick leave and one bucket of hours for Vacation—you're going to love it!

The truth is that you don't really have to love it. You can even say, "this is kinda dumb." But if you want to be noticed for the right reasons, it's a good idea to get on board, tell others it's not that big of a deal (it's really not), or that this change is a good thing, and we just need to accept it and move forward.

How you react to changes will be noticed. Again, the rock-solid pick-six bet certainty in your career is that the landscape will be continually changing because managers around you, above you, and below you will be trying to make changes. Some changes will be for the better others for the worse. In general, those that can readily adapt to change, respond to change, and possibly even lead change will be the ones that thrive. Those that recoil from change, that put their head in the sand, that hide in their cubicles doing what they have always been doing and hoping that the change will go away, or at least never cross the threshold of their precious, personalized cubicle space—their careers will suffer.

The fact is that when change happens, there tend to be two groups. The first group is those that are part of the "problem" (which may not even truly be a problem). They represent the "old way" of doing things. The second group is those that are part of the "solution." These are the people who are willing to embrace the "new way" and help lead the charge. We think you know which side of the equation you need to be on.

What if the proposed change is a bad idea? For the most part, the sorry answer to this is that it doesn't matter too much. Chances are, by the time you hear about the idea, it is a foregone conclusion and the time for debate and substantial modification has long passed. Perhaps something a colleague named Pete said years ago will give you some solace. Upon hearing of one of the company's latest "innovative" changes, he promptly noted, "All companies are brain dead; it's just different parts of the brain!" The change that is making you think, "I gotta get out of this nuthouse and get a job at Google," is probably a change that originated with a disgruntled Google employee tired of the crazy changes that inevitably happen there too and looking to get into your industry!

The point is that change happens in every company in every industry. Unless this change is going to unleash nuclear missiles and cause WWIII, we suggest you trust the leadership of those proposing the change and do your best to get on board as fast as possible and see how you can be part of the solution. When a change is announced in a public office meeting, you do not want to be the spokesperson for the naysayers, questioning the wisdom of the decision. You want to step back, take a deep breath, listen hard, and jot down any questions you have for future discussion on a one-on-one basis with your boss and/or other people in charge.

Here's a recent example. In an effort to cut costs, David's company instituted a "hoteling" program for the office. Since David and many of his colleagues were on the road much of the time, and much of the office space tended to go unused during many of the days of the week, the thinking was the company could save some overhead dollars by reducing their office space by roughly one third, eliminate personal offices, and have everyone share the remaining spaces by reserving the space ahead of time just like a hotel room.

The merits of this type of action have been debated in workplaces across America. (And it may seem like it flies in the face of the section later on "working less from home," and you'll think we're nuts.) The point here is that this was a significant change. Here you had people that had been with the company for twenty-plus years, that had worked their way from cubicle land to their nice cushy offices full of personal items such as pictures, awards, favorite photos, hunting trophies, sports memorabilia, and other non-work mementos. Beyond the personal space changes, there was also the new behavioral changes required to book space ahead of time and pack up things into files and storage at the end of the day so the office "hotel room" was ready for a new potentially different employee the next day.

The reactions to this change were classic. You had several early adopters that packed up their offices the next week, they talked about how much money this would save the company, how this was a change that was long overdue, and the company was now a lean, mean, modern machine. Then you had others who waited until the last possible moment to clear out of their spaces. They happened to be out of town on "deadline day" to remove their stuff, so administrative staff had to do the bulk of their office packing. They complained about missing files, about the flaws in the office space reservation system, about how hard it was to find a private place for a phone conversation, how their personal productivity had decreased substantially during the change, how the office space looked impersonal and generic to clients that walked through, etc.

The fact is that both camps were a little bit right, and everyone in the company had a choice to be on one of these teams or the other. In the end though, the ones who embraced the change were smiled upon by management, and the gripers for the most part exposed themselves as a bit old and stodgy (even if they were not "old"—they came across as "old"—and not in a good way) and resistant to change. None of their complaints amounted to any change in policy or behavior.

Our point is that you will have lots of these types of change response "opportunities" ahead of you, and you will have a choice how to respond. Don't be part of the problem. Be part of the solution.

BE EASY TO TALK TO

· · · · ·

"The only thing that will redeem mankind is cooperation."

—BERTRAND RUSSELL

When Simon was managing teams, there were many occasions when he had to get important messages out to everyone. These messages were not only important, but they were also sensitive enough that they needed to be delivered personally—ideally in person but at least over the phone and not by a mass email. It was on these occasions that Simon found that he learned a bit about his relationships with his staff because he knew who the easy calls or meetings would be with and knew the calls he was dreading. He knew who he wanted to call first since he always liked to make his first calls to the people with whom he had the best relationship. Simon also knew he probably wouldn't have his delivery perfected until after two or three calls, and he needed to talk through his thoughts a bit without risking getting crucified for saying the wrong thing to the wrong people.

"There were some calls that I always saved until the end. Before dialing the phone, I would take a deep breath, make sure I had enough time on my calendar to listen to all the questions and concerns and complaints and worries and fears that would no doubt be unleashed on me." These people may have had their strengths that enabled them to keep their relatively important jobs, but they often had a weakness which was that they did not let news or change roll off their back easily. They did not give their managers much breathing room when it came to decisions that might impact them. These were the same people that would respond to any group email directing a slight change in policy with either an immediate phone call demanding their own personal explanation or an email "reply to all" challenging management's thinking with a long laundry list of concerns, clarifications, and suggested improvements. Again, these people had their strengths and this same attention to detail and passion expressed itself in many positive ways, but darn were they challenging to deal with sometimes!

What does that say about Simon and his staff? That his approach, while perhaps a bit cowardly, is probably typical of many managers. Most people do not relish conflict, and it's always going to be tempting to procrastinate or even avoid these tough conversations. Who has time for this? Most of the time a boss just wants her staff to get in line, say "Okay no problem. I'll do my best," and then go forward and get it done.

After several years of seeing this kind of range of behavior among staff members, it finally dawned on Simon that he could drink a bit more of this Kool Aid himself. He had to ask himself—am I making it easy on my boss to talk to me? Do I let news roll off my back a bit and follow direction without complaint most of the time, or do I contest every policy change and directive? Because Simon wanted to be easy to talk to, he decided to spend a little extra energy to work on this trait. He consciously made an effort to hold himself back from commenting all the time to try to show how smart he was. He put focus on being a good listener and trying hard to understand his boss's predicament. This resulted in the boss coming to him a bit more often during challenging times. By showing a bit of respect and empathy for his boss's position and maybe even tossing in some humor to make him feel better about the tough decisions he had to make, made it easier for her to come to Simon and allowed him to gain much more insights into his boss' position. He wanted to be the person that his boss wanted to call, not the person that she dreaded calling. Not only did this put Simon in good standing with his boss, but it helped him in his personal preparations for the next level up in the company.

When You Become the Boss

This same quality of being "easy to talk to" is going to help you in your management role when the time comes. While one could argue that you should not be too approachable for your staff to bug you about every little thing and demand individual explanations for everything, We think this quality will help you much more often than it will hurt you. Do you want to be the kind of boss that rules by fear and your staff don't ever want to come in and talk to you about anything bad for fear that you will lose your temper and blame the messenger? While this might seem nice at times since you will not be bothered as often, this will come back to bite you in the end. Some issues will blow up before you have a chance to control them, staff will leave before you have a chance to intervene, clients will get bad quality service without you knowing, etc.

You want to be the kind of boss who staff think of as easy to talk to. Your staff need to feel comfortable coming to you as issues are developing to talk things through. This might be an issue in their family that they are worried might impact their job performance, or it might be news about an unhappy client, or news that a bunch of staff are not happy about some recent shift in corporate direction. If you are not hearing about these things early, then you are not on top of your business and you will not succeed.

You cannot possibly know everything that is going on in your group if you are not easy to talk to. It is up to you to set the tone of a true open-door policy, and you will need to coach your staff continuously on the types of issues you want to hear about immediately and the types of issues you want them to handle on their own. And when they do come to you, don't bite their head off, or they will think twice the next time.

RAISE YOUR HAND AND VOLUNTEER

• • • • •

"If you can dream it, you can do it."
—WALT DISNEY

A simple fact about any business is that there is always more to do. Lots of tasks get left undone at the end of every day. Many strategic initiatives are not acted upon because there is simply only so much time in the day and most people's to-do lists are already too long to get through. This leaves a vast amount of opportunities for the ambitious career climber to raise their hand and volunteer to take on some tasks that others are not getting to and start making a difference for their company.

Volunteering is an outstanding way to get yourself noticed and separate yourself from the crowd of employees that are just trying to make it through the day and collect their paycheck. Volunteering tells your boss and others that you are able to handle your own job and then some. You are ready for the next level, and you are willing to do whatever it takes to help the company. This is a very positive and strong message.

Now don't forget that you first have to be able to do the job you were hired to do. Don't volunteer for new tasks if you are already under scrutiny for handling your "real job." You need to take care of this first. But if you have your real job pretty much under control, and perhaps even have the ability to delegate some tasks to others to carve out more time for yourself to grow into other duties, then by all means talk to your boss about other areas where you might be able to make a difference.

Notice that we said talk to your boss. (It has to do with that chain-of-command thing everyone needs to learn if you're working in corporate. It's as inevitable as death and taxes). You can't go all rogue and volunteer for things all over the company without your boss knowing about and approving your plans. Remember, bosses have interests of their own as well, and your volunteer efforts might best be served for their purposes—helping them look good for their boss(es).

Think about how you are "volunteering." Are you jumping up in the middle of a meeting to volunteer like a third grader who just figured out the answer or a character in a Saturday Night Live Cheerleader skit? Are you grudgingly saying, "Oh, okay, I guess I could do that, maybe, kinda, sorta … Okay, well, you can count me in if no one else wants to do this, I guess …" Perhaps you should consider the professional way to volunteer when you are in a meeting and the boss asks for volunteers. A simple, "I'd be happy to do that" works pretty well. You can talk about the details with the boss later. Of course, if you are a cheerleader type, then you be you. Otherwise, I suggest you proceed like you've been in the end zone before.

Once you start listening for them, you will see that volunteer opportunities pop up all the time. In your boss's weekly meetings, or in some presentation by a visiting senior manager, you will start hearing sentences such as "Later this year we hope to start analyzing our clients for their buying tendencies," (maybe you can help them start doing this now!) Or "we are going to start rolling out this new IT system across the company," (maybe they need local experts in each office to help people learn the new system!). Or even as blatant as, "we are looking for a few volunteers to help out at the client function planned for next Saturday." (Hello!)

One of Simon's favorite early volunteering stories was when he was about one year out of college and his company was preparing a big proposal that needed to be mailed to Cincinnati for a Monday deadline. The team had been working nights all week to finish this proposal targeting a Saturday morning FedEx deadline. When Simon walked out of the office Friday night, he joked with his boss that he was available to hand deliver it if it came to that. Sure enough, Simon got a call at home Saturday afternoon taking him up on his offer and asking if he could get on a plane the next day to Cincinnati to hand deliver the proposal since the powers-that-be couldn't make the FedEx deadline. Simon jumped at the task, (that was back in the days when travel was a fun novelty anyway) and when the client selected his company for that project, Simon was mentioned personally in every company announcement as one of the heroes that helped save the day and win the big project! Simon knew his role was fairly minor (and actually a bit fun), but it was a big help to others, and it made a bit of a name for him around the office.

Look around for some things you can do to help the cause—above and beyond your real job. You will get points just for offering, and you will build your reputation as a loyal, dedicated employee that has capacity to take on more and more responsibility and authority.

Raise your hand today!

Do Both

• • • • •

> *"If to do were as easy as to know*
> *what were good to do, chapels had been churches*
> *and poor men's cottages prince's palaces."*
> —WILLIAM SHAKESPEARE

Time conflicts and overlapping assignments are a regular part of life in the corporate world. If you haven't experienced this existential conundrum already, you will have many occasions where you will be asked to do important tasks or favors for important people even when you have already committed your time and energy to other assignments. How you handle these occasions of conflict can potentially make or break these valuable opportunities to make an impression.

Often these personal-time infringing requests will start with a question such as, "Do you have time to … really piss off your girlfriend by breaking plans? Would you be able to … do this long boring thing I couldn't be bothered to do? Could I ask you to … eat this old break room croissant for dinner since you're going to miss the reservations with your now very angry girlfriend? To which you should answer, "SURE."

Simon has a clear memory of a time about five years into his career when he had just started working directly for a Senior Vice President of his company. The VP was located in another office so Simon's dealings with him were irregular and infrequent and often via email, which is how the VP dealt with everyone, including people who sat in offices or cubicles within a thirty-foot radius of his office. Simon's role at the time was to provide an internal service to various other Presidents and Vice Presidents of the company. "And as you can imagine, there were often times when I was pulled in several directions at once by these powerful people who were each very used to getting their own way."

On one such occasion, Simon drafted a long but logical email explaining this conflict to his new boss—something about one VP needing him to do one thing and another VP needing him for another at the same time. "In the moment, I thought it made for riveting reading. In the email, I carefully weighed the pros and cons of each request, described each request in detail, considered which was more important for the company, which was more convenient for me, why I might or might not want to do each one, etc. I then asked my boss to prioritize this conflict of timing, essentially solve my problem."

The boss's response: "Do Both."

The subtext was "go away." A key thing you need to understand with your boss is that they have more on their plate than you do; they are not looking for more problems to solve.

Simon was pretty shocked in the moment, but it was a good lesson in growing into a company asset. As part of the structure of a company, you need to be self-supporting and have your responsibilities under control so that you are free to support your boss and your team. Sometimes striking this balance takes creativity, but sometimes it just takes time management. The hour he spent constructing that obituary for his promotion could have been spent working on one of the two conflicting assignments!

Remember that work assignments or requests from the boss don't always come at a good time. You might be about to walk out the door to meet a friend when you get that "Hey, have you got a minute?" summons into his or her office. You might have just made plans to get away with your still-angry girlfriend to a microbrew craft beer festival. You might have just taken on another assignment that is going to take up a lot of your time. On these occasions, keep all of that personal conflict slamming around in your brain to yourself and agree, agree, agree. Once you actually hear out the assignment, you'll be tempted to tell your boss that it falls under someone else's job description. You might know a coworker who would be a better fit. It could be too complex, it could be beneath your pay grade, it could be intensely boring and terrible, and none of that matters. Empty your head of logic and be a corporate drone in a Dilbert comic for one second, and answer, "Of course."

This saying-yes policy will not ruin your life. Often, things aren't as dire as your boss, or your imagination, might make the task out to be. You can typically negotiate time frames, negotiate quality, engage your peers, work longer hours, work after hot yoga, work after dinner, work after you argue with your girlfriend about the hours you work. In most cases, you can find a way to put in the extra effort.

Let's start with an axiomatic position that you need to adopt, "Do what you say you will do, and do it when you say you will do it." Make a commitment and keep your commitment, with respect to both what you promised to produce and when you promised to produce it. We've adopted this as our personal mantras. Saying yes and keeping your commitments need to become part of your personal brand. Honestly, you don't really have a choice. You don't want to be known as someone who can't deliver on time. That would be very bad mojo for you. Short-term conflict that turns into long-term success is just one more good investment in your corporate future.

TAKE REVIEWS SERIOUSLY

• • • • •

"My what a wasp-stung and impertinent fool art thou,
tying thine ear to no tongue but thine own."

—WILLIAM SHAKESPEARE

We all think we are pretty good at what we do. Confidence is a beautiful thing. It's vital for all of us, but it doesn't mean we should be arrogant about what we are doing, and it certainly doesn't mean that we can't do better. We need to learn to listen to others around us, particularly at performance review time, to help us identify areas for improvement.

David sat down for a performance review early in his career with his boss and the boss above him. "I felt like I was doing a great job and was one of the shining stars of my group (confidence bordering on arrogance). I was quite confident that I was going to get a heaping measure of praise and adulation from my boss."

"Well," the boss said, "you're doing fine, and I think you should join *Toastmasters*."

"My brain is now racing. Who did he think he was talking to? My speaking skills were, in my opinion, really, really good and I was too stunned to say anything. The review lasted about fifteen minutes, and I left the office deflated."

What, indeed, was the thinking? David asked his boss exactly that the next day, and the boss relayed that he had an opportunity to hear David speak at a technical conference where, in his opinion, David was underwhelming as a speaker (and "underwhelming" was being generous—he was flat out terrible at that conference). "Fast forward three years later to the previous day's performance review, and this was the only constructive criticism that he could come up with. At least he'd put the effort into trying to think of something constructive to give to me."

As it turns out, the boss was right. "I did need to get better as a public speaker to grow in my career. And the boss was also wrong because he hadn't taken the time to work with me during the previous twelve months."

Lessons learned? Sure, a bunch—let's start with David, the reviewee.

"My over-confidence (I didn't think I was arrogant which probably just proves that I was indeed an arrogant jerk) caused me to not take the review seriously. I never sought out constructive criticism. I never chatted with my boss about what I was doing. Never sought his advice. Never discussed project or personnel issues with him (note, "personnel" not "personal"). I never asked for input as I simply didn't think I needed it."

Whether or not you think you are doing a great job—whether or not you think you need input—*you need to seek input. You need to seek ongoing performance reviews, and you need to take it seriously.*

We talk with clients all the time about continuous improvement programs and actually implement such programs for clients from time to time, but we recommend that you have a personal continuous-improvement program for yourself. Not that you should be in your boss's office four times a day asking, "How's this; am I doing what you asked for?" like David did as a student intern, "which drove my boss at the time nuts—he didn't know how to tell me to stay away." What David should have done is check in with his boss weekly or biweekly to tell him what was going on and to *seek advice.* Then, when the annual review came up, there would be no surprises, and the boss could give his young intern constructive criticism that's a bit more comprehensive.

One other way to help out your reviewers is to give them a couple of references. Mention some people that you have worked with closely and can give them a different perspective of your performance. If you are really gutsy, you may also ask them to speak with a client about your performance. (Simon did this once when he knew he had completely exceeded the client's expectations on a specific project assignment.) Good reviewers seek multiple perspectives, and you can help your boss do this.

When you eventually become the boss, you will need to be doing reviews. We know we're looking ahead here, but if you reverse engineer this, you will see what you can be doing now to help your boss help you better.

So what if you are the reviewer? If you have responsibility for a team of people, you should go out of your way to speak with them frequently about what they are doing and how they can do better. You, as a supervisor or manager, should take ongoing reviews very seriously. This is a very significant aspect of the job of any supervisor or manager. David tries to talk with his direct reports as often as possible. One of them has a standing biweekly, one-hour "touchpoint" meeting with him. One calls him about once every three weeks to give him an update on what she is doing. One schedules monthly calls with David, and, "We all talk as frequently as we can to keep our business moving forward by making sure that we, as a team, are working in sync and that everyone is doing what is expected of them."

When review time comes around, reviewers do talk about past performance, and Simon strives to provide constructive criticism that is real—for everyone involved. In almost every case, the constructive comments are ones they have already heard throughout the year. Simon strives to use the majority of the time to talk about career growth (even if their career aspiration is to take his job) and personal growth (things that this team member can do to advance his or her career and build skill sets necessary to advance).

When both take it seriously, performance reviews are no longer a chore but an opportunity for a fruitful discussion and personal and career improvement.

READ THE MEMOS

• • • • •

"I never direct myself, because I don't like
working with me. I would punch me in the mouth
if I had to take my direction."

—RON PERLMAN

One of the things that blows us away about young professionals today is the intense amount of effort that they exert to do things outside of work. It's really very impressive that you have the time and ability to maintain a thriving latte art travel blog, compete on the national indoor bouldering circuit, and lead a neighborhood composting initiative. Don't stop doing this stuff. It's good stuff, and we elders are a bit jealous that we missed out on the joys of playing in an ultimate frisbee league.

We can tell you that personal computers and knowing how to use all of the features on your smart phones have gifted you hours in your day that didn't exist before. You have the amazing ability to Google a list of restaurants, Yelp some quick reviews, verify these reviews with Instagram photos, make a reservation on Urban Spoon, and Lyft to the door of the most authentic Korean fusion restaurant in town.

Time has expanded in a way that arguably we haven't seen since your everyday citizen stopped farming. Let's be honest. We're jealous. Seriously. Do you know how many hours we spent troubleshooting a typewriter in our early corporate days? There is no turning a typewriter off and back on again as an annoying, but simple fix; you need a box of tools, and you get hard-to-remove ink on your hands. Copy and paste, autosave, spell check, and BACK SPACING, did not exist! We think of how many hours we've spent doing things in our careers that now take seconds, and it's honestly a bummer. It is really hard for most people of previous generations, even the kicky and happening ones like ourselves, to admit that technology has offered up for free what we had to struggle for.

But we're also pretty good at math, and we know you absolutely have hours to spare.

You may be thinking that we are going to use this section of text to suggest that technology is bad, and so are you, so go throw your smart phone off a cliff. Far from it. So here's the problem: everyone we talk to is so busy, no time to spare, barely making deadlines, and yet the problem seems to be less a matter of time and more a matter of priorities. This whole book is predicated on the idea that you want to be successful in your corporate climb, that you want to be promoted, well liked, and contributory. This is why it's important to make the time to read the memos.

Corporate communications come in many forms, annual reports, financial statements, memos from senior management, web presentations, blogs, personal presentations, and more. They are not always useful or timely or clear, and in most cases, they may not appear to have any relevance whatsoever to your working life. We know this for a fact because we have both composed our fair share of these difficult-to-read corp-speak missives. That said, make a point to read these memos and reports, and attend the shareholders meetings and presentations when you can. Try to think through why certain decisions or policies were made. If you're asking, why bother? The answer is pretty simple. If you want to be at the best advantage for success, you need to stay in alignment with senior leadership and the rest of the company.

Most of you do not have day-to-day contact with the CEO or other senior leaders of the company; these communications can be your best window into the direction of senior management. Who cares? Look, it's up to you to try to row in the direction that senior management is pointing towards. If you don't read the memos, and you don't know that reorganization is occurring, or a new advertising campaign has started, or that a new branding strategy is underway, then you can't row in that direction.

Aside from making yourself an informed member of your company, you should read these communications in order to help make your immediate supervisor look good. We will say this many times over the course of this book; you will go far if you act as a support structure for your boss. You will find that your boss is flooded with even more information than you, and it may be harder for him or her to stay up to speed with various corporate communications. Reading the memos will help you stay in front of change, allowing you to adjust your course in advance.

When you first start out, you have very little, if any, ability to help steer the corporate course of direction because you really don't have any pull anyway. As an employee you have the responsibility to try to do a good job interpreting vague directions coming down from the powers on floors above. Something you should understand is that, typically, corporate communications discuss new policies at a fairly high level with the details left outstanding. It is left up to middle management to interpret the policies as they see fit. If you take it upon yourself to keep up with company communications, no matter how boring and distant the information is, you will be putting yourself at an advantage.

When we suggest investing in this bank of corporate information, we immediately get complaints that young professionals are "mUCH TOo bUsy" to fit more into their workday. To that we say, *no you are not* (and if you don't believe me, read the first part of this chapter again). When we say to keep up with this stuff, we don't mean that you need to take notes and study over the Vice President's initiative to boost sales that will ultimately be scrapped by next week; we just mean be familiar. Skim it, keep up with it, in the same way you scan your weather or news apps. It's about having a baseline reading on what's happening; you don't need all the details. You can look through company performance numbers while you are in an Uber or Lyft. You can listen to the archived stream of the shareholders meeting during your gym time. You can browse HR emails while you wait in line at Starbucks when you forget to order on your mobile app.

This goes way beyond just reading the musings of some senior executive who is ruminating over the latest corporate "flavor of the month." Your colleagues communicate via email for group functions ("we're all meeting for happy hour"), items of interest to everyone (baby announcements or engagements), or corporate stuff that needs emphasis (the bosses say everyone only needs to work a half day on Friday). Just read the memos. In David's group, they organized a weekend get-together, and he offered to get Chinese food for everyone. He put this in an email to the group and someone else emphasized it and made some suggestions for other food and drink items that people could bring that would be appropriate with the Chinese food he was procuring. People offered salads, fruit plates, beverages, and Swedish meatballs. That was not on the list of "appropriate items." You have to read the memos!

You can keep up with the vitals of your company. You just need to make it a habit. We guarantee that, as it builds little bits of information into your understanding of your work world, it will pay off. Taking the initiative to stay informed on changes, up to date with company direction, will impact the way you are perceived. This investment of time will allow you to have informed opinions and worthwhile questions, and when you invest in your company, more often than not that investment will have a return.

GHOSTING
(A.K.A. MINIMIZE WORKING FROM HOME)

• • • • •

"80 percent of success is showing up"

—WOODY ALLEN

"Personal relationships are the fertile soil from which all advancement, all success, all achievement in real life grows."

—BEN STEIN

It's important to show up—particularly earlier in your career when you are building your brand. Part of the art of getting noticed is to let people see how committed you are. That means you are *there.*

Regardless of the fact that the world runs on Skype, and conference calls, and emails, and texts, and everything that can possibly cut down on human interaction, there is value in existing in physical form. It is a super simple equation; your boss will like you better if he can establish a relationship with you in person. There is just something about face-to-face interaction that can't be replicated remotely.

Don't complain that you are available, that your boss can reach you, that you are a real self-starter time-management wizard. It doesn't matter. The opportunity to shine is often in social interactions that are only possible in person. Maybe one day you casually talk out a problem with a grumpy client, and they happen to mention to your boss how they liked you. Or perhaps accounting is looking for a bunch of missing receipts, you randomly find them in a trashcan, and your boss is there for that big save-the-day moment. It doesn't matter what luck-based thing places positive associations next to you in your boss's mental "employees who don't suck" chart, they will count in your favor. Do not become the Where's Waldo of your office, a ghost who haunts an empty desk intermittently and doesn't know anyone's name.

Because we are both "The Boss" now, we realize that this may be our problem more than it is yours. Maybe we should be a bit more flexible. That's true. Maybe we could adapt to your way of doing things. You can probably get stuff done while riding your electric scooter around town. But back to the "as a boss thing." As a boss, we can tell you with great certainty, *"mi problema es su problema."* If the boss can't get behind your afternoon paddle-boarding escapes (hopefully you work by a body of water so that you can engage in this outstanding activity) then you've got a problem.

It also doesn't really matter what other people think is the best thing to do or what the studies show. When you are working hard to climb the corporate ladder, we would argue that you need to suck it up, get out of your house, and be part of the team at the office.

Yes, there are several tempting arguments one can make against this advice. If you want to work from home, you may choose one or more of these arguments to state your case. We, however, are here to disabuse you of each of these notions:

1. **The environmental argument.** You say, "commuting is such a waste of gas and resources." You can take public transportation, a van pool, or do a ride share—problem solved.

2. **The efficiency argument.** You say, "I am so much more productive at home without all of these people barging into my office and distracting me." Naw—C'mon now, you're talking to me. I occasionally work from home and there are way more distractions at home than in the office. The daily newspaper, the coffee pot, getting the right station on my Sonos, checking to see if the mail came, etc. Don't buy this one.

3. **The daycare argument.** You say, "I need to be home to look after the kids since my spouse works too." Hold on now. We know that people, at times, need to work from home because they have a child who is ill and can't go to day care or school. We've stayed at home with a sick kid and know you can't get anything done because you are taking care of your sick kid. And if your child isn't sick, you've probably plopped them in front of the TV to watch Disney movies on an endless loop, which are also a significant impediment to getting work done. On this one, you need to Let it Go!

Now there may come a time when the stigma of "not being at the office with the rest of us" will diminish much more than it has already. But we would argue that the business world is still far from this time, particularly in large companies, and the perception is that the stay-at-home workers are more interested in their personal quality of life issues than making the company successful. And you know those people you say are distracting you? They are really trying to work with you because part of your job is it collaborate with others in your office. So, are they really a distraction or are you just being antisocial?"

Someday technology may enable conference calls and video conferencing to be much more like "being there" than it is today. Someday you'll have a robot that runs around your office as your personal representative. Right now, however, remote conference call participants are still much less effective in meetings than those that are "in the room" and they miss much of the value of the in-person meetings and social connections that occur in the minutes prior to and after the formal meeting.

Plus, it can simply be an annoyance and a distraction dealing with the technology issues of trying to accommodate the people that have dialed-in for the call. How many meetings have started with the first ten minutes being wasted to make sure the remote people can see the computer screen of the presenter, or if they have received the file that was just handed out at the meeting, or trying to describe a sketch that someone in the room has just put up on the white board. We would put the value of the remote participant at about 60 percent of the people in the room. Multiply that by fifty meetings per year and you get a sense of the diminished effectiveness of being remote.

If you want to give yourself the best shot at career success, you need to be available to kismet. We know that may not vibe with you because the world should be a meritocracy with a completely unbiased level of fairness. Yes, it most certainly should; but that is not reality. You need face time, not Facetime, in your work life. This is the most basic aspect of working in most companies: You will have to get out of bed, and put on clothes, go to work, and talk to your boss. Listen, the gods cannot collude in your favor if you are biking in the park during a conference call with your Bluetooth headset on mute. All it takes is an impromptu question to derail your whole professional bent.

Here's a dirty little secret that the bosses have—when we look at our business and try to figure out if we could be more efficient and effective. Question #1 is "What are these remote employees doing?" Question #2 is a little more disturbing: "Do we really need them?"

When was the last time you saw an announcement from a major corporation that read like this: "Joe Smith, who has been working from his house for the last four years, will be returning to the office to lead the company's North American Division … ." ?

WHEN EVERYONE IS A GHOST

• • • • •

*Even fools are thought wise if they are silent
and discerning if they hold their tongue.*

—BIBLICAL PROVERB

When the President of the United States, the governor of your state, your CEO, or your boss says that everyone is working from home, then the rules of "ghosting" are changed. This situation can be caused by a worldwide pandemic or by a natural disaster such as a fire, earthquake, tornado, or flood. Things can happen, and when they do, they happen fast. So the best thing for you to do is to be prepared to know how to deal with working from home in a way that's productive, collaborative, and positive.

For some people, working from home is easy. They lock themselves away in their working space and just get stuff done. For some, it's more difficult. Kids, pets, roommates, significant others, newspapers, and other distractions keep them from being as productive as they'd like to be.

Notwithstanding your level of productivity, the thing that will get you the most notice is how you deal with conference calls. We have some thoughts on this based on many weeks of working from home during the 2020 COVID-19 pandemic.

Your clients and your coworkers will engage you in conference calls or video conferences, and like other opportunities in your working life, these are opportunities for you to shine. We think it boils down to what you say, and in the case of video conferences, how you choose to present yourself.

What you say matters. You have to find a way to meaningfully participate in conference calls. It's tough because people are scrambling to say things, talking over each other, talking while they are on mute, and saying dumb stuff when they think their mute is on. It can be a free-for-all, but you, young Jedi, don't have to fall into that trap. Here are some suggestions:

- Know how to operate the particular conference/video call system you are using. This means know how to go on and off mute, how to be on video (or not), and how to share your screen. It's not hard to figure this stuff out. Practice with a friend or a family member if you need to.
- Be on time and smile and greet people when greeted with a friendly hello, good morning, good afternoon, or some other socially acceptable phrase.
- Stay on mute if you don't have anything to say or if it's a call where others, like your boss, are just telling you what's going on.
- Prepare for the call as much as possible. If it's an internal call, then you may think of questions you'd like to ask or be prepared to talk about what you are doing on a particular project. If it's a call with a client, then be prepared to discuss your part of the project. A pre-call with the client team before you get on the call with the client is often worthwhile to make sure everyone knows what everyone is going to say. Don't wing it. No matter how good you are at extemporaneous speaking, this is not the time to go free-form. Usually those who do fit nicely into the "fool" side of the dichotomy presented in the proverb noted above.
- Don't be a suck up. Don't feel like you must reiterate what your boss said or tell your client what a genius they are. This is completely transparent to everyone on the call including the person who you are trying to impress.
- When you are talking, please try to make sure that any background noises you can control are not noisy. What noises can you control? Radios, stereos, washing machines, dishwashers, your cell phone text-notification sound, and whatever twenty-four news station is to your liking. Keep them off if you can.
- Load up a decent headshot of yourself into Microsoft Teams, Webex or whatever system you use. It's nice to see a smiling face inside of the blue circle or whatever mechanism indicates the individual who is talking. Be careful with your headshot. Put something in that is relatively recent, has a plain background,

77

and is not a selfie. Get someone to take the photo (in portrait mode if you are using your phone) if you need to. Don't put in a photo of you with your significant other, your pet, your mountain bike, your surfboard, or any other animate or inanimate object. This should be only you.

When you are on video, there are a few additional things you should consider.

- Dress appropriately. This doesn't mean you put on your Christian Dior suit. It means that you wear something two steps above your favorite Jethro Tull concert tee shirt that you bought on Ebay. Put on something decent, comb your hair, and present yourself like, at a minimum, you would on casual Friday.

- People can see behind you on the video. Even if you can blur out the background, people can still see. Keep it neat. It doesn't have to be barren, just tidy. Try to keep the kids and pets and other distractions out of the picture. This may seem funny to some but can be quite distracting and annoying to others.

- Don't go video mode if you don't have to. It's not necessary for small groups or quick conversations. It can be distracting. Some people don't have enough bandwidth to have a clear video image and that can be more distracting.

This is all part of the continuous evolution of business and business practices. Make sure your skills are up to speed for the zombie apocalypse. And don't forget to stock up on toilet paper as well.

BEING RIGHT VERSUS BEING HAPPY

• • • • •

"Part of the happiness of life consists not in fighting battles, but in avoiding them. A masterly retreat is in itself a victory."

—NORMAN VINCENT PEALE

Simon once had a boss who used to always use the line: "Well, do you want to be right, or do you want to be happy?" It took Simon years to fully understand what this line meant, and now he seems to see its applicability everywhere he looks. We've actually started to use this line a lot ourselves.

The idea is that you don't need to win every argument with everyone, or prove that you are the smartest one in the room all the time. In fact, being the smarty pants all the time and not letting discussions die until you win can often work to your disadvantage. Sure, you may prove someone else wrong and walk away feeling pretty smart and high on your horse, but what about the other person? They might walk away thinking you are a real jerk whom they don't want to do business with or help in any way in the future. Now are you glad that you won that one? Everyone is going to be a lot happier, including you, if you just keep your mouth shut and let things drop once in a while.

A classic example of this that we still laugh at to this day was when David's project team had just heard word that we had won a fairly significant victory in a large competitive bid for a multi-year project. A day or two later, our boss's boss sent out an email congratulating the team. The only problem was that he got just about every fact wrong that he possibly could including the name of the client, the name of the project, the amount of dollars involved, etc.

Most of the team had the same reaction David did, which was to smile at the errors and at least be thankful that we were being recognized by the company for a job well done. Except one guy. Yup, you guessed it. He had to send the smarty pants "reply all" correction email that had nearly zero positive impact but had the unspeakable dual negative impacts of embarrassing this company big wig who now was effectively called out as being out of touch, and making everyone on the "reply all" distribution aware of how naïve and self-important this smarty pants guy was.

Another example of this is politics. There is an unwritten rule in most business settings that you don't introduce politically sensitive topics with clients or even your boss or your peers since there might be too much risk of being on the opposite sides of an issue and thus setting up a barrier between you and that person that didn't exist before. There is simply too much to lose and too little to gain with these types of conversations. And if political topics do come up in conversation, this is an excellent time to keep the "being right versus being happy" rule in mind, and focus on listening and trying to understand their point of view rather than feeling the need to impose your views on them and win an argument for your political view point.

You should never be the one to correct your boss in a smarty pants "reply all" message or in a client meeting or in a group setting of any kind. You should never be the one to try to win a political argument with a boss or a client. Your bosses are going to get their facts wrong. It's just one of those facts of life. If you feel there is a compelling business need to correct them (not just your own personal sense of what is right and wrong), do so in a polite, private way that allows them the time and space to figure out whether the mistake warrants a public correction of any kind. Taking this approach might earn you points with your boss for your maturity and discretion, rather than damaging your relationship had you taken the smarty pants route.

You and the Boss—Last Looks

Understanding Them is really about understanding how You and Them can work together through the daily grind that starts sometime in the morning and usually ends long after 5:00 p.m. in the evening. It starts with the understanding that everyone is looking at you like a prizefighter entering the ring and understanding that every jab, every punch, every feint, plays into how your personal brand is viewed.

The good news is that you can control the narrative. You can write the story about this prizefight called a career. You have to understand Them just like the fighter understands his opponent. You play to your strengths, and this is where the prize fighting metaphor falls apart, you help your opponent (also known as Them) play to their strengths as well.

What do you get out of your understanding of Them? You get the ability to figure out how You and Them can do more than merely coexist. You now have the ability to create Us. That is where you'll find your happy place. Understanding Them gives you the ability to determine how the decisions You make, at every inflection point in your career arc, can impact your brand. When you learn to work together effectively with Them, you will build your brand in the best, most positive ways.

THREE

You and Your Team

Leveraging Your Brand

YOU ARE YOU AND THEY ARE THEM. YOU WILL THRIVE WHEN YOU understand how You and Them become Us. That's the place where you have figured out how to successfully deliver for Them, work with Them, make Them happy and positively impress Them. In other words, it's "how to play nice in the sandbox."

At the same time, You can develop the balance in your life that you desire and build the career path that you want to be on. You plus Them equals Us. "Us" doesn't mean that you automatically have more time for your family, friends, or surfing (both the ocean waves and the internet varieties). It means that you have found the way to take the things you do best and make you the most satisfied and develop those into a strong brand that has a positive impact on others in your working sphere of influence.

This is really about your daily interactions with your teammates, your approach to work and life, and your ability to disagree with others in a way that doesn't make you disagreeable. It's also about how you deal with difficult situations, how you have honest interactions with others, and how you deliver for the people that need you to deliver—your clients, customers, bosses, stakeholders, and you know how this list goes by now. Over decades of working with the nicest, meanest, craziest, weirdest, smartest, kindest and bluntest people on the planet, we have some thoughts, that we are sharing with you, on getting to Us.

KNOW YOURSELF AND YOUR TEAMMATES

• • • • •

"What we have to do ... is to find a way to celebrate our diversity and debate our differences without fracturing our communities."

—HILLARY CLINTON

When you are young, communication is easy. You think that everyone thinks the same as you do, and therefore they should react the same as you do to any situation. Anyone who doesn't understand you or react the same way that you do is simply an idiot and not worth worrying about. Does this remind you of any teenagers you know? How about any managers in your company? Ahh, ignorance is bliss sometimes ... .

As you advance in life and in your career, you start to realize how different everybody is, and how hard it is to please or motivate different types of people. You gain a much deeper appreciation for diversity and the importance of recognizing these differences (more in personality than in appearance or cultural heritage) in order to communicate effectively to your team and eventually lead or motivate large or even small groups of people. You also start to realize that you have your own personal behavioral quirks and oddities that tend to fit various psychological behavioral patterns, and you might not be as perfect or even as uniquely brilliant as you thought you were.

If you have never taken any of the personality or behavioral style self-assessments (examples include Myers-Briggs, DiSC, FIRO-B), you should find an opportunity to do so. Attempting to understand yourself and your own styles of behavior will help to give you insights you never imagined into understanding others around you. It's like discovering a set of tools that other people have been carrying around all along for understanding and fixing situations in the workplace, when up until now you have only been using your bare hands.

One we particularly like is the FIRO-B assessment, developed by Dr. William Schutz in 1958, which assesses people across three areas of interaction with others: inclusion, control, and affection. The idea is that people have different needs and wants for **Inclusion** (how much you generally include other people in your life and how much attention, contact, and recognition you want from others), **Control** (how much influence and responsibility you need, and how much you want others to lead and establish procedures and policies), and **Affection** (how intimate you are with others and to what extent you want others to approach you for deep personal relationships).

Simon remembers the first time he took one of the FIRO-B as part of a three-day group training course. It was like a new door opened for him to changing the way he perceived the people in the world around him—both at work and at home. (His wife always gets nervous when he comes back from these training courses.) A few of the early takeaways:

- I am not perfect (surprise!), and I am vulnerable to these same classes of needs and wants in order to be happy, just like everyone else.
- Other people's "needs" for happiness are different than mine, so they do not react the same way as I might to various situations.
- Understanding these needs is central to my being happy as well as to effectively leading, pleasing, or motivating others.
- Great team members have a sense of self-awareness and understand the strengths, weaknesses, and needs of themselves as well as their teammates for inclusion, control, and affection.

What Simon really found interesting—and comforting—was that he got to see that his boss was a person too. "He had needs for affection, inclusion, and control (well, I knew that last one!) just like everyone else."

Arm yourself with this awareness about yourself and the people around you, and we promise that the world will start making a little more sense to you. Did you ever wonder why you were so irritated when you found out that you were not invited to that meeting last week? Or why you were so much more comfortable with last year's strategic plan when you actually were included in the process of developing it? Or why just a few words of encouragement from your boss can make all the difference in the world to your willingness to work next weekend? Or why your boss was so thrilled to be invited to join you and the team for happy hour last week? Now you know.

BRING ENERGY AND PASSION

· · · · ·

"Nothing is as important as passion. No matter what you want to do with your life, be passionate."

—JON BON JOVI

If you were to talk to leaders in your company about the characteristics that separate the good from the great employees, chances are that energy and passion would be in the top five on everyone's list, if not number one. You will find that the people that rise to the top are the ones that consistently bring energy and passion to their job every day. This is usually not an act. They love what they do, and so they care about the little things and the big things that are going to make a difference in the company success, and it shows.

This is why it is so important to find a job, or at least aspects of your job, that you love to do. When you love what you do, bringing the energy and passion is easy to do every day. It is not an act. It is fun. Your energy and passion become contagious, and you inspire others to bring that same energy and passion to the tasks at hand. With your passion, the whole team can rise to success, or at least to a much higher level of performance than otherwise possible. The people who do this are usually pretty easy to notice, and increasing levels of responsibility, authority, and compensation tend to come their way.

If you are like most people, this is easier said than done. When we think of passionate people we tend to lump them in the same category as

86

Cheri Oteri and Will Ferrell doing their *Saturday Night Live* Cheerleader skit—shamelessly positive people with lots of "school spirit." If you do the cheerleader thing to get noticed, you are essentially the same as the guy wearing the purple and green peacock feather headdress running through an airport not in the City of New Orleans and not at Mardi Gras—unnecessary and inappropriate. Passion and energy are mostly just being positive about stuff in a good way. It is not about making people gawk at you. Let's explore that difference a bit more.

Passion is being positive about what you are doing and seeing the benefit in what you are producing. If you are making widgets, passion would be understanding how the widgets are used and provide benefit to society. If you can think of what you are doing in that way, you can likely gin up some passion about your work.

Energy means that you put your foot on the accelerator a bit more than you might normally like to. You walk with purpose into meetings with a smile on your face rather than with your head down staring at that Facebook post on your phone that you've already read three times. It means that you are pleasant and positive to others, that you strive to see the positive in what you are doing both individually and collectively, that you positively and as enthusiastically as your DNA will allow participate in company functions and events. That's not so bad, is it? No cheerleader outfits. No inspirational exercise breaks ("C'mon everyone, let's stand up and stretch—please don't bop your neighbor in the head"). That all seems doable, doesn't it?

Yes, it's doable most days. There are, however, times when you like what you are doing at work and times when you don't. There are days when you feel like raising your hand and volunteering for that unpleasant but potentially important assignment, and days when you don't. There are weeks and months when you are thinking more about the next vacation, the weekend activities, and your 401K balance than the next sale or next important business process improvement that is going to help the company bottom line. You can't control these feelings—they are real, and they are the truth.

Simon's own career has been full of three- to five-year arcs where for the first year or two he was excited about the new area of work or new geography that he was working in. It was easy to bring the energy and passion, and he was able to make a substantial impact on the business area he was in. He then found this excitement begin to wane typically by year three, and if he didn't find something new to work on, he would suffer through many months struggling to bring the same level of energy and passion that he knew he needed to truly excel at the job. Sometimes life gets in the way and the timing is not always right to make a move within the company or to another company. Sometimes the business itself or overall economy is not offering enough opportunities to easily switch business areas or move jobs. Sometimes you have to grit it out even when the job has become a bit boring or business opportunities seem sparse.

Looking back, Simon realizes it probably took him too long to recognize when he was hitting those periods where energy and passion were hard to come by. Had he been more self-aware earlier in his career, he would have recognized what was happening and made shifts earlier to keep himself more engaged, passionate, and happy. He thought he was the only one that got bored after a year or two of doing the same thing, so he kept his thoughts to himself and hoped things would get better or new opportunities would come his way.

The reality is that some people who are desperate for success will try to fake the energy and passion a bit more than others if they want to succeed. This can work for a while, but the problem with this faking is it's not fun, and in the end, you won't possibly be able to sustain the energy and passion levels at the level of the people that truly love what they do. You will burn out because faking is hard work. Let's be honest with ourselves and realize that if we are faking it, we are lying about ourselves and ultimately, we'll get found out. That can be dropped into the "very bad" column of your career-growth spreadsheet.

A better course of action is to seek out areas of the business that you enjoy and possibly even love, and try to delegate the tasks you don't enjoy, or move away from the business areas in which you have trouble raising your energy level. This is where self-awareness is critical. You need to face the fact that your success will be limited if you are not genuinely passionate about the work you do and the line of business that you are in. There are other people that will love that same work more than you do, and they will be more successful because they will try harder and be happier and bring more energy and passion than you. And it will show.

Look for your sweet spot in the business where bringing the energy and passion is easy and real. This is not always easy to find, but when you do find it, you will also find greater success.

GUARD YOUR PERSONAL LIFE TACTFULLY

• • • • •

> *"Beware the barrenness of a busy life."*
> —SOCRATES

This is a tricky one. For some employees, the work-life balance is like the holy grail, something that you are always striving for but you never quite achieve. You always want either a little more money or a little more personal time—if not a lot more of both. On the flip side, the management of your company may pay lip service to wanting you to be happy and have a personal life, but in reality they mostly just want you to keep your mouth shut about your family and get the job done, including late nights, weekends, whatever it takes. Of course, there are exceptions to this, but you will be better off if you operate with this assumption as you encounter each individual work-life balancing decision.

This gets even more challenging when you have a family at home, because then the late nights, the weekends at the office, and the long business trips are no longer just about you, but also about your responsibilities as a spouse and a parent. If you struggle with this, you are not alone. Take a look at the senior management of your company. Odds are that many of them have been divorced one or more times. To get where they are, they probably didn't put their family first too many times.

To add to the challenge, this is also a changing landscape and every company is likely to be different depending on the makeup of the senior management team. Many of the older workers in the workforce today came up through the ranks at a time when family came second, no one whined about a work-life balance, and thus they maintain an attitude that says, "Hey, I put in the hours when I was young, why can't you?" However, companies are also realizing that the younger generation is not expecting a forty-year stay at their current company and talent could walk out the door if they're not coddled a bit.

Okay, so there is no right answer and single solution to this issue. Now what? The trick here is to have some core values that you live by in a consistent manner (notice we said "consistent" not "rigid" here!) and keep the following messages in mind to help you navigate your work-life balance:

1. **Know Who You Are and Who You Want to Be.** Your CEO asks you to attend the corporate weekend retreat on the same weekend that you have a major family reunion planned. How you handle this kind of conflict depends on who you want to be. If you want to run the company some day and that is truly a realistic option for you, you might need to do the corporate retreat. Otherwise, you might want to take a pass on this weekend and enjoy your family.

2. **Keep Track of Emotional Bank Accounts.** In his *7 Habits of Highly Effective People*, Stephen Covey introduces the concept of an emotional bank account. These are the "chips" that you have either loaned or borrowed from your spouse or your boss or your kids when you either do something nice and giving (investing in the account) or you ask for favors or forgiveness (withdrawing from the account). Knowing what your "balance" is in each of these accounts that you have with different people in your life can help you with your decision making. For example, if you just spent the last two weekends doing corporate duties and perhaps landed a big sale with a new client, you may have invested nicely in your emotional bank account with your boss, but you have been taking withdrawals from your family account and that balance might be dangerously low. The family account will need more investment soon, such as by attending that family reunion next weekend ... .

3. **Get on the Same Page and Communicate with Your Spouse and Your Boss.** This is the corollary to keeping track of your emotional bank accounts. You need to have honest communication with your spouse about who you are and what kind of role you want in your company so that he or she knows why you may or may not be devoting your extra time and energy to work rather than family occasions. You need to understand and be sensitive to where your boss is coming from and communicate with him or her appropriately. If your boss has no life outside of work, then chances are he or she isn't going to be too sympathetic to your personal life. If there is a significant misalignment here, then you might want to find a different boss to avoid endless struggles over this issue.

4. **Pick Your Battles.** Keeping track of your emotional bank accounts and having a solid relationship with your boss and your significant other will allow you to pick your battles with each side and get closer to the elusive balance you are striving for. Take advantage of times when there are not a lot of family commitments to invest in your work-related emotional bank accounts. Work those weekends or late nights when it is relatively painless to do so, such that when the time comes when there is a pressing family engagement calling you've earned enough chips to cash in and take some time away from work. At the same time, when you are with your family you need to "be there" with your family. Don't be that person who is always on their cell phone all weekend or vacation rather than spending quality time with your family. This is a lose-lose situation where you are doing your work and your family a disservice and withdrawing from both sets of bank accounts at the same time.

5. **Be Tactful.** Don't say dumb stuff. We'll illuminate that point with an anecdote. Simon was once in charge of a relatively small consulting group with the corporate mission to sell and deliver projects throughout the USA. With only a handful of people and a national geography to handle, they had to travel for nearly

every sales opportunity and project assignment. The people in this group knew what they were getting into when they signed on to this group, and travel was simply the cost of doing business. You can imagine how surprised Simon was when he was holding an annual performance review with one of the staff members in his group who opened the discussion with "My number one goal next year is to not get on an airplane." Really? Your number one goal? And that's how you want to start your performance review?

Simon had to catch his breath and pause when he heard that one. A statement like that speaks volumes, and there is almost too much going on in there to address in this book. Let's just say that there was a significant misalignment here between person and role, and even though this guy was an outstanding employee in many respects, he was clearly struggling with work-life balance issues and he decided to take a rather tactless and aggressive approach to letting his challenges be known.

As a boss, despite Simon's sensitivity to work-life balance issues, this statement was not helpful to him and his own mission and responsibilities to the company. It merely presented him with a problem to solve without a clear solution. A more tactful approach for the staff member would have been to start by discussing some his business goals for the year and the things he enjoyed about the job, then communicating in a clear but non-aggressive manner that travel was becoming a bit of a strain for him. Perhaps then the staff member could have asked if Simon had any ideas about how he might be able to contribute to the company in a significant way with a little less travel. This would send a message that he values the company mission and wants to contribute, but he needs to find a more sustainable role in order for him to be successful. Do you see the difference?

So, as you strive to find your perfect balance, you will want to pick your battles and opportunities to thrive in each environment, and remember to be present in the environment where you are. Don't just create problems for your boss or spouse by abandoning one ship or the other, but rather help find replacements for yourself to ease the burden of your absence. (And we think it goes without saying, but we're going to say it anyway, that those replacements should be more towards the work-related side, at least until they perfect cloning.) They wouldn't call it a work-life balancing act if it were easy, and if you ever figure out a simple solution to this issue please let us know!

USE PLAIN LANGUAGE

• • • • •

"If you talk to a man in a language he understands, that goes to his head. If you talk to him in his language, that goes to his heart."

—NELSON MANDELA

"The data schema is cross-referenced with the asset performance SQL database insofar as the critical KPIs are concerned." This could be a random bunch of words assembled into a sentence as part of a party game. Or, it could have meaning to someone. It may actually be profound. We just don't know. We likely would not deign to interrupt the utterer of this strange group of nouns, verbs, and acronyms to say, "I have no idea what you just said—can you please repeat this in plain English?" Maybe we should build up the courage to ask the question because we are quite positive that most people hearing this sentence are not quite sure what it really means.

Why do people use crazy technical language and acronyms in their everyday speech and not just use plain language? We think the reason is that language becomes the secret handshake that gains one access to the speaker's secret world. If you understand the terminology and the acronyms, you get in the door and can have a conversation. If not, then sorry, you can't enter into the secret world of information technology, finance, high-level business, engineering, medicine, or whatever it is that the discussion is centered upon.

A colleague (who frequently uttered sentences similar to the one above) was tasked with developing an Information Technology offering to take

THE RIGHT START: *Build Your Brand to Survive and Thrive in Corporate America*

to clients. His speech was laden with acronyms and technical terms. As someone in a business development role at that time, David wanted to know exactly what the techie guy wanted the company to sell and exactly what benefits the client could derive from this service offering. David could never get there—nor could anyone else.

David worked to understand all of this guy's technical terminology and acronyms. David even asked someone to show him a "data schema" on paper. "Okay, now I get it." David was constantly asking his colleague to supply case studies and benefits of his concepts. David could never wring this information out of the guy. Some executives in the company thought this colleague was a genius, yet as David says, "and I, with my stegosaurus sized brain, could never comprehend the genius issuing forth from the lips of Mr. Acronym/TechieTerm. Other executives agreed with me. They told me, 'I don't think this guy knows what he's talking about, and he's using all of these terms to cover the fact that he has no idea what our clients want or need.'"

After about eighteen months, with no significant client interest in his service offering, this individual became a "former colleague" as executives realized that he really didn't know what he was talking about—despite the use of some genuinely impressive technical terminology.

As engineers, we're familiar with scientific terms. As David says, "When I go for my annual physical, the doctor I see strives to speak in plain English but his training sometimes pushes him to use technical terms. Normally I understand these, but when I don't, I ask for clarification. I want to understand what he is telling me." When someone gets into "crazy talk" mode, ask the person for clarification. You'd be surprised how many others have no idea what someone is talking about.

As an aside, you should know that it's appropriate to ask for clarification. While we're talking about you using plain language in dealing with others, you should know that "others" might not use plain language in dealing with you. So, ask them what they mean. Ask them what the acronyms mean. Ask them to give an example. This is particularly critical when someone is defining what they want you to deliver to them. Don't "think you get it." Ask questions so you can actually "get it." You may ask a question, and

94

then repeat what the Techie Termer said in plain language. Don't be shy in asking questions to understand what you need to do.

The smartest people can explain very complex topics in simple, plain English. Ridiculously smart people like Carl Sagan, Albert Einstein and Stephen Hawking have this skill. I have seen clever CEOs like Jack Welsh and Steve Jobs explain what they do without ever resorting to "biz speak." You are a smart person—explain it so your mother or father would understand it!

You Don't Always Have to Agree

• • • • •

"If everyone is thinking alike,
then someone is not thinking."
—General George S. Patton

An extension of this loyalty concept applies to how you treat people in larger meetings or group situations. We're big believers in being honest and speaking our mind. We are obliged, as members of a team, to have thoughts and opinions about our business, our clients, our employees, etc. We've learned the hard way that if there is a good reason for not agreeing, then you should not agree and you should make known your concerns.

The trick about not agreeing is how you go about this. Most people don't like to be embarrassed in public. We don't know anyone who actually does like being embarrassed. Therefore, we try to never embarrass anyone in a public meeting by saying they are wrong or disputing what they are saying. Here's what we've found to be helpful: if appropriate, you might say, "could we look at this another way" or "could I add to what you are saying." In other situations, you need to be either showing support for your team or keeping your mouth shut.

If your boss or a mentor of yours says something at a group meeting that you disagree with, this is not the time to raise your hand and question their intelligence or judgment. Plan to have a private discussion with them later.

This will show your respect and loyalty for them, and avoid a potentially embarrassing or career-limiting moment for you. If you are asked for your opinion then you should give it. If you disagree with what is being said and you can respectfully offer your dissent in a public forum, then do so.

The same goes for email. Unless you are praising someone for a job well done, or demonstrating your unbridled support for a new initiative, perhaps you should consider picking up the phone or getting off your rear end and walking over to your colleague's or boss's office for a one-on-one conversation. In any case, we suggest that you avoid the "reply all" option at nearly all times. If you have some concerns to raise with one of your advocates, you don't need to show this to everyone. Take a deep breath, think about the risk and reward ramifications of what you are doing, and then either approach them directly in person, on the phone, or in a polite direct email.

WHEN YOUR TEAM CAR
BECOMES A KLOWN KAR

• • • • •

"If it is possible, as far as it depends on you,
live at peace with everyone."

—THE APOSTLE PAUL

Things are going great. The metaphorical team car is clicking on all cylinders—couldn't be better until someone morphs into a Killer Klown from Outer Space. They offer scathing criticism of others or they simply imitate Mount Kilauea and start spewing hot ash and lava. Now the team is in a tail spin. You are bickering or outright fighting with teammates. No one wants to go out and get dinner. Things are going off the rails. What happened and what can you do to return to being the idyllic team from Kansas.

What causes someone to blow up? Lots of things could have happened. Bad news from Dr. Ruth. Their cat ran away. They didn't take their meds. It's a full moon. Weezer cancelled their tour date in Keokuk. The convenience store doesn't have quadruple IPAs in stock. Doc Ock just crushed Spiderman. We could go on, but we think you get it. Sometimes people just have brain spasms. Something happens in their lives—could be relatively inconsequential like the IPA thing or it might be very serious like getting bad news about a mortgage application. You don't know. They may tell you, and they may not.

If you sense someone got some bad news or is just having a bad day, please try and have some grace for them. Many times the volcanic eruption is pretty embarrassing to the individual, and they want to leave Planet Me and rejoin Planet Team at the earliest reasonable opportunity. You can try and take them aside and let them talk to you. You can give them some time alone. You can take a break as a team. Perhaps there is someone on your team whose Emotional Intelligence quotient is higher than yours—they are usually the person to try and help the individual. Don't ignore people in these situations. They are more often than not looking for a sympathetic ear.

The reality is that the isolated eruption and consequent temporary explosion of team unity is infrequent. More often, the pressure caused by a difficult task or project delivery deadline reveals someone's true character. It's probably revealed your character more than you'd like to admit.

When things go sour because someone you thought was a good person is really a jerk, it's a much more difficult problem. Sometimes the boss is needed to solve the issue. Sometimes the problem is the boss. Whatever the case, in our experience, the best thing to do is to keep moving forward.

Perhaps your colleague, Krakatoa the Younger, will rejoin you—perhaps not. If they are really a bad person, then you may not, as a team, achieve your goal. Perhaps they'll go and complain about you or another teammate to your boss. Perhaps they'll start gossiping and trying to turn teammates against each other. Perhaps they'll start making insulting, personal jokes about another teammate under their breath in the meeting. Perhaps they'll storm out of the meeting room to go and find that elusive IPA that they are craving. Maybe they'll plop themselves in your cubicle with the explicit intent of keeping you from doing your job. Maybe ... go ahead and fill in the blanks from your own experience. You've seen it happen.

We don't understand the psychological pathology of Klowns. We can only offer some suggestions to deal with the Klowns that are borne of personal experience:

- You can ask someone who is disruptive in a meeting to stop or to leave. It's best if the meeting organizer or facilitator does this. Shame has a powerful effect so asking the Klown who can't keep their mouth shut to "shut it" often shuts them down.

- You have the right—nay the responsibility—to tell the Klown to immediately desist if they insult other people, other races, other religions, other genders, etc. Saying nothing or having amnesia about someone's completely unacceptable behavior is complicity. This might be something that we learned from your generation. Seriously, you're right about this. Thank you.

- If someone gossips about you or complains about you, the very best thing to do is to just keep doing your job and keep good notes about your interactions with others. A colleague once complained about David's work performance to his boss. "We were working on an odd technical issue that required us to collaborate and share our findings. This particular colleague claimed that I had not completed my share of the work. That was true—I had not. I did, however, have notes indicating that I'd asked this colleague three different times to share his work with me so that I could complete my portion of the task, and each time, this so-called colleague claimed that he didn't have anything to share with me. Our boss got it and pushed this Klown to give me what I needed so I could complete my work that evening (yup, I had to stay late). I should have gone to the boss earlier and outed this Klown by asking for a progress meeting so that his treachery could be revealed—my mistake."

The advice to try and live at peace with everyone works for us—and it's worked for a lot of people we know and have worked with. We may not be particularly successful in this endeavor because the world is an unstable place occupied by people who tend to be unstable. But it's worth trying, and we can tell you from vast experience that we churn a lot less stomach acid when we try to take this approach to dealing with the Klowns out there.

How to Handle Kriticism from a Klown

• • • • •

The truth you speak doth lack some gentleness,
and time to speak it in. You rub the sore
when you should bring the plaster.

—WILLIAM SHAKESPEARE

Criticism is often tough to handle. Public criticism from a smug jerk is indigestible. You have to recognize that people who do this are simply trying to make themselves look smarter at the expense of someone else. We're calling this "kriticism." They use pretentious language and offer their critiques as if they were developed through brilliant psychic communication with Freud, Socrates or Einstein.

A 1981 Brandeis University study by Teresa Amabile called "Brilliant but Cruel" notes that the individual offering criticism of others often does this so that they appear to be smarter than their own personal reality. The study notes that "pessimism sounds profound and optimism sounds superficial."[1] There you have it. Your colleague is trying to escape the "optimism trap." Yeah, we know that there is no such thing. We do know, however, that most people see business endeavors as a zero-sum game—there's a winner and there's a loser. It does not have to be this way. It should not be this way. You are wise to the pessimist's wicked scheme. Here are some thoughts on how to handle this kind of "kriticism."

- You can simply offer to explore the other person's idea without defending your own. This is simply a deflection technique to kick

---

1   Teresa Amabile. "Brilliant but Cruel." https://files.eric.ed.gov/fulltext/ED211573.pdf

the can down the road so you can have the discussion without having the "jury of peers" listening in on you. The criticizer, with no one left to impress, may then engage in a reasonable discussion with you. You don't have to be defensive, even if they are dead wrong and you are totally right. The gracious thing to do is to say something like, "Let's explore that later." If they still disagree with you, then you can agree to disagree and move on. You can't please everyone.

- If criticism is valid, even if it's delivered by a total Klown in a total Klown way, then take the advice to heart and do a better job. We're both totally turned off by Klowns (really, who isn't), and we are also always learning to be better at this ourselves. When David ran the Southern California operation at his company, his boss had a big regional meeting in a Las Vegas hotel with about fifty managers and corporate staff from around the US. "My group had a bad quarter and my boss was pounding me about this on a daily basis. At this meeting, in front of my peers, my boss decided to make an example of me by shaming me about my group's performance. Then, he had one of his corporate staff who was and still is a Klueless Klown do the same thing. Valid criticism delivered in a really mean-spirited way."

"During the Klueless Klown's soliloquy on my performance, I got up, left the meeting room (yes—everyone saw me leave) and went into the bar. A few minutes later, a peer named Jeff came and sat next to me at the bar and didn't say a word for a reasonable period of time. Then, he looked at me and said, 'You probably know that there is a waiting period when you try to purchase a gun in Nevada.' I didn't know this, but he was basically telling me to chill out and come back to the meeting. At least I think that's what he was saying and that's what I did. And as for the criticism—yes, they were right. I should have foreseen some issues and done a better job. And I probably could have taken it with a bit more humor and laughed it off: 'Yup, I know I gotta do better, thanks to all of you for letting me know and repeating it again and again and again.'"

- If you can rationally and reasonably defend yourself in the public meeting, then do so. You do have to be careful as the evilest criticizers bring half-fact/half-truth to their argument. The best ones will have some fact or bit of information that you did not know, or they will take some inconsequential fact and make it the cornerstone of their argument. If you are a great debater, then this is your opportunity to shine. If you have honed your public discourse skills on the mean streets of any of New York's five boroughs, you are very likely to be able to take down this Klown Kriticizer. If you've never been on the debate team or you are not New York five-borough-trained, it's probably best you pick option 1—"Let's do this later," or option 2—"I'm going to take this with good humor, tell this chump that he/she is right, and then deal with it later."

FRIENDSHIP ... OR NOT??

• • • • •

"The best thing you can possibly do
for a friend is to be his friend."
—PIERRE ELLIOTT TRUDEAU

Hopefully you have noticed that we are trying to take a very positive spin on each element of your climb up the ladder. You should have learned in Kindergarten what it means to be a friend. We won't rehash that for you because you already know.

Sometimes the appropriate positive behaviors are best illustrated by some negative examples. These are things that friends don't do. You shouldn't do these to your friends, and if people do these things to you they probably aren't your friend. Many of these behaviors are unavoidable—people are people, so you will see these in the workplace. Your job is to recognize these behaviors—these negative behaviors—and make a decision to rise above the fray and do NOT behave this way. Here are just a few examples of team and interpersonal behaviors to avoid:

1. *Backstabbing.* This is criticizing others behind their back. If it's valid, say it to them in person. If it's negative, say it to them in private. If it is trivial, be a grown up and keep it to yourself.

2. *Gossip.* Spreading rumors about others—often their personal behaviors—is unfair, unkind and just dead wrong. If you are in the habit of doing this you will end up making yourself look foolish. If the gossip you are spreading makes someone look bad, you are sinking to their level and making yourself look bad in the process. Avoid the gossip.

3. *Fake Friend.* Be aware that most of your work friends will be just that—work friends. These are people that you have friendly interactions with at work, but they are not your real friends with whom you share a lot of personal stuff. Of course, it is possible to have some real friends at work—but be careful. Sometimes work friends can be fake friends that may extract personal information out of you, stuff that you tell real friends, and spread the information to places you do not want it to go.

4. *Fake inviter.* Hey, we should get lunch sometime! Come by my office any time to talk! Many times these can be sincere invitations, but many times they are not. Beware the fake inviter who wants to be a fake friend. On the flip side, if you make an invitation, be sincere and follow through.

5. *Braggart.* You do not need to talk about your accomplishments. No one wants to hear it. Let your actions speak louder than words. Praise from others will come in due time. We're always amazed by the Facebook or LinkedIn post that starts with the sentence, "I'm so very humbled to receive this prestigious award." Nope, there's nothing humble about that.

6. *Wind bag.* Don't go on and on about your commute or your airplane travel delays or your party weekends on the shore, especially when you have just arrived at work and others are

trying to concentrate. No one wants to hear it. If they care, they will ask, maybe over lunch or outside the office.

Every day you work as part of a team to deliver for your company and your clients. Be a great teammate. You'll never regret having someone say, "You were a pleasure to work with!"

BE LOYAL

· · · · ·

I'll take fifty percent efficiency to get one hundred percent loyalty.

—SAMUEL GOLDWYN

This may seem like a little thing, but the fact is that loyalty in the corporate world can be a big deal and you need to be mindful of this issue. There are going to be times when the people who helped you get to where you are will need—and expect—your full support. You know who these people are. They are the ones that hired you, or supervised you for several years, or helped you get a key role or position, or maybe even just counseled you as a mentor when you needed some advice.

These loyalty "opportunities" can come in all shapes and sizes. You might be asked to assist your boss to stay late and analyze a bunch of data and prepare a bunch of unusual spreadsheets during a time of corporate upheaval to help her look good for her boss. You might be wooed by a mentor of yours to join his group when a division is splitting into two and you need to pick which ship to sail on. You might get asked for a favor by one of your mentors to host someone from out of town for dinner, or to pick up the tab at some client function that might look a bit excessive on your next expense report, or to sit in on a meeting that he or she cannot attend. These things might be a bit annoying and come at a bad time for you, and be a bit embarrassing to explain to your spouse, but usually when you are being "asked" for these favors, they are not really asking, they are expecting a bit of payback for the favors they have done in the past or could do for you in the future. The same concept applies with peers and subordinates. They may need you to help them out and your ability to support them is loyalty.

Another aspect of loyalty is what you say to others. Loyalty means that you do not gossip about your teammates or say negative things about them to others. "Damning with faint praise" is a very easy trap. The interesting thing is that the colleague who you "damn" almost always finds out about it.

David recounts the following story: "I was working on a project on the East Coast and I told the president of my division that I wanted to fly home over the weekend for a long-planned family event. He gave me his approval. Two years later, when I was being considered for a promotion, I found out that a colleague who had been working on the same team had told the Division President that I wasn't committed to the success of our company as evidenced by the fact that I flew home for a couple of days in the middle of this project. I reminded the Division President of my situation and his agreement, and I still got the promotion. I haven't forgotten what was said, and it changes the way I interact with this individual. I don't know why this person said this and they were not a competitor for the promotion. They had their reasons. It didn't feel loyal to me."

One more thought about loyalty. Loyal team members stick together. They share the glory for successes, and they hang around when things go bad. President John F. Kennedy said, following the Bay of Pigs disaster in Cuba, "Success has many fathers, failure is an orphan." Loyalty demands that you stay part of the team in times of success and failure.

Many years ago, the firm we both worked for pursued a major contract that involved people in our organization all the way up to the C-Suite. We did not get selected for this contract, and the mid-level executive who was in charge of the pursuit told several team members that he was "leaving the blast zone." He was going to take ZERO responsibility for the failure of the effort. In fact he turned into a revisionist historian as he claimed to have minimal involvement in the effort. We think the "leaving the blast zone" comment is really clever—but totally wrong. It's a low character move. Another mid-level executive who stayed loyal got blamed—that was unfair. The first guy rose up through the ranks and then flamed out at several high-level jobs with our company and several other companies. The other person was a loyal employee who had a very successful career in our company. Karma.

CROSS THE FINISH LINE HOLDING HANDS

• • • • •

"Individual commitment to a group effort—
that is what makes a team work, a company work,
a society work, a civilization work."

—VINCE LOMBARDI

Not everything you do is a competition where there is one winner and a bunch of losers. And for clarity, not everyone gets a trophy even if everyone wins. In most business endeavors, there are no trophies. Often the best you can hope for is a thank you. Many business activities require group efforts and sometimes these activities require collaboration with other business entities within your company or outside your company. We think the "win-win" approach is a better outcome than "you win—everyone else loses."

Our firm was competing for a large project. The competitive process required that David's group work cooperatively with another group so that we could offer comprehensive services for the execution of the project. David remembers, "The other group manager came to me and asked how I would like to negotiate with him with respect to splitting the sales costs and dividing up the potential revenue. I told him that I'd negotiate with him after we won the job. I preferred to put all of my energy into winning the job rather than working out internal details of no consequence to the competition. I told my colleague that we'd be able to work it out because I believe in 'crossing the finish line holding hands.'"

The Special Olympics is a competition for developmentally disabled youths and adults. They train and compete just like anyone else. Many Special Olympians, however, aren't out to crush the competition. There have been instances where, in a race on the track, a Special Olympian falls and the race leaders stop, retreat to where their competitor has fallen, help pick him or her up, and then continue the race holding hands, ultimately crossing the finish line together. In this case—everyone is a winner.

Why does business have to be a zero sum game, a game where the number of winners are balanced out by the number of losers? We don't believe in the zero-sum approach to business. Rather, the Special Olympics approach—an approach where everyone is a winner—is by far the better way to go. By this we mean that you don't overtly compete with your peers. Go out of your way to support their efforts. We have both learned the value of going out of our way to help a colleague be successful in such a way that no-one gets credit. Sometimes the "bosses" find out about this, and sometimes they don't. It doesn't matter. We're in business to help our company help our clients be successful. Nothing gives us more pleasure than to deliver a project or work product for a client that meets or exceeds their expectations.

Don't fight with your colleagues. There is more than enough competition for you with other companies in your market space. If you want to compete like a cage fighter, you can certainly do that with external competition. Collaborate with your colleagues, work together, support them to deliver excellent products to your clients or customers. Most of them will remember you as the person that they can completely rely upon to do the right thing for your clients and your company.

You and Your Team—Last Looks

The corporate game is a contact sport for which there are very few rules. Perhaps your company offers you the URL for their on-line employee manual. Great—now you know how to fill in an expense report, but you don't know the game plan for working together and getting ahead. You can make your own game plan—one that focuses on tactfully, smartly, nicely doing the things that get you noticed. Baseball legend, Reggie Jackson, referred to it as, "the straw that stirs the drink. " What he meant by this is you can be the person who holds the team together and moves things forward. You can be the person who has figured out how to get along with the wide swaths of personalities, work ethics, and communication styles that comprise the team—your team.

Along the way, you can Krack the Klown Kode and figure out how to deal with the nastiest predators in your group. You can also figure out how to work with your boss and be a team player who doesn't always agree with every syllable that your boss utters. Just "don't ever do it in front of the troops," as Rich warns Kim in *Better Call Saul*. Smart team players know how to play nice in their corporate sandbox while still delivering. Smart team players are budding leaders who are building a brand that will get discussed in a very positive way by the bosses while they are out on their corporate golf retreat.

PART TWO

THRIVE!

FOUR

You at the Helm

Deliver What You Promise

A S YOU MOVE FORWARD IN YOUR CAREER, YOU WILL FIND "TRICKS-OF-the-trade" that make your life easier and make you stand out in a positive way. These tricks are really tools, systems and mental models that will help you evolve from the person taking orders to the person leading the team in the way that you would like to be led. They help convert You into Us.

We learned about these tricks and tools the hard way. We didn't know about them or use them when we were in the first few years of our careers. They would have been useful then. They are useful now. They will be useful to you. Some of these tools are simply mental models, such as always working to prepare for meetings or activities where you will be called upon to speak or lead. Some can be technology-based tools, such as systems.

Some tricks are combination plates—your system will change as technology evolves and being a life-long learner will help you keep up with these technological advancements. We want you to be prepared. We want you to be committed to the success of your team, your company and your career. Most of all, we want you to have some insights into our failures and successes so you can take the right path as your career evolves and grows.

PREPARE

• • • • •

"Failing to prepare is preparing to fail."

—JOHN WOODEN

There is no argument that John Wooden was a very successful basketball coach and leader. He led the UCLA Bruins to ten NCAA men's basketball championships in the 1960s and 1970s. His team had an eighty-eight game winning streak. He started coaching at UCLA in 1948 and that was his second head-coaching job. Coach Wooden wasn't all that successful in his first job at Indiana State where, fun fact, he was both the basketball coach and the baseball coach. John Wooden figured out how to be successful and it took him a few years—like about seventeen—to reach the pinnacle of success in his profession and win a national championship.

Coach Wooden published something called the "Pyramid of Success" which sets out his philosophy for winning at basketball and in life. There are many things that one can learn from John Wooden, but we like his concept of being prepared and there are two stories that really illustrate this.

The first story is about practicing so that you are the best you can be at "game time." In the mid 1960's, before UCLA had won their first championship, one of the assistant coaches, named Jerry Norman, prevailed upon Coach Wooden to install a particular defensive scheme known as the "zone press." In this scheme, UCLA players would apply pressure to the opposing team in the backcourt to try to steal the ball and score easy points. The UCLA players practiced this defensive scheme daily. Coach Wooden wanted them to be prepared. They had one unusual facet of their practices in that they never worried about what the other team might do to counteract the zone press. They simply practiced to be the best they could be at the zone press. There were even occasions when the UCLA players did not know who they were playing that evening and had to send a team manager out into the arena to get a program. Coach Wooden did not want the players preparing for the other team. He wanted the players preparing, practicing, and perfecting the zone press—let the other team worry about UCLA. This worked out well for Coach Wooden and the Bruins. They scored a lot of easy points as a result of their zone-press system.

The second story has to do with details. One of the first things Coach Wooden taught his players on the first day of practice was how to tie their shoes. He did not want one of his players to have an untied shoe during practice or games, so he told them what he wanted them to do. They practiced his shoe tying methodology until they got it the way he wanted, and then they moved on.

Applications seem obvious—practice before you play and every detail counts. Can't argue with that. Here's the problem for non-athletes: we don't square off against an opponent for forty minutes in the basketball arena. We play every day—meetings with clients, meetings with our bosses, one-on-one sessions with people on our team, working on work stuff. Sometimes there is no opponent in sight—it's just us.

Why is preparation so important? So many reasons, but let's just look at meetings for a start. You call a meeting with your team to discuss an important issue. Everyone shows up on time with their laptop and a cup of a coffee or tea—brewed with fair trade, non-GMO beans or leaves, of course. You start talking about the issue. No agenda, jumbled presentation, unsure of some concepts. It's a waste of time. You didn't prepare, and you didn't get up to speed on the details that were necessary to help you and your team come to a decision.

In the professional services world, this happens all the time with our clients. How do we know? We've both had clients tell us directly, "Don't ever send that guy out to see me again." Why do they say this? It's because our guy was unprepared and did not have a sufficient grasp of the details that were relevant to the client.

Wait a sec—you're a smart person, you can talk about anything your company does, you can "wing it." You walk into the client's office, politely accept their offer of non-fair-trade-brewed-more-than-two-hours-ago coffee and then ask, "So what's keeping you awake at night?" *No*—you didn't just do that, did you? That's so twenty years ago. You can't say trite, trivial stuff to your clients. You need to be prepared and be there for a reason and that reason has to be to try and provide some benefit to the client.

We both can tell you that most of the one-on-one meetings that we've had with clients in their offices have been to solve problems, deal with personnel issues, talk about difficult technical issues on a project, and then go out to lunch. In every case, we had to get prepared, and that preparation involved input from several others as well as a discussion about what we might say to the client about the thorny issue and how we would like to solve it. It's extra work for sure, but no one likes having their head handed to them by a client, so it's definitely worth the time to prepare and dig into the details. David has a good strategy. "Once we have the info, then I actually practice, with others, what I want to say to the client. I want to get it right and have a productive meeting. I can only do that by being prepared and paying attention to the details."

GET DEFINITION

· · · · ·

"If you aim at nothing you will hit it every time."
—ZIG ZIGLAR

You can't deliver something if you don't know what you are delivering. Again, even the simplest of tasks have some type of "scope" by which they are defined. You have to define success to achieve it. You have to get definition on a task to deliver that task. How do you do that? You have to ask. If you don't know, you have to ask. If the person requesting the task is unclear in their instructions, you have to ask. If the fire alarm goes off briefly in the middle of this person explaining what they'd like for you to do and you miss just a smidgeon of their explanation, you have to ask them to repeat it.

Most people are fine with you asking for better definition. They don't want you to waste your time, and their time, by doing something poorly and having to redo it. If you can't think of any questions when you are given an assignment, at least say to the assignor, "I may need to come back to you and ask some questions as I figure this out." That isn't so hard, now, is it?

Let's dig into task definition, or scope if you prefer. There are three things that you have to know to define a task and we'll look at each one.

- The first is what do you want me to deliver?
- The second is when do you want it delivered?
- Finally, (and this doesn't always apply) how much do you want to spend on this?

You should start with "what." What do you want? What should it look like? To whom is it going? What is the level of quality you are looking for? Can you give me an example? What is it to be used for? You can probably think of a bunch more questions to ask. Many times—in fact most of the time—you will have the answers to most of these questions without asking because you will have done similar tasks for others. You should, however, think of the task in these terms. What am I being asked to do, and what is the purpose of this deliverable?

Purpose is a very important element of the task scope. It will give you insight into what you are doing and enable you to better understand how to deliver a useful "deliverable." When in doubt, ask. If your boss berates you for asking (some bosses can be jerks, remember), just say you are trying to deliver excellence to them, and you need them to help define what excellence looks like. If they refuse, then find another boss-level type person or a peer who has done it before to help you scope out your deliverable.

Always strive to deliver excellence. This can be a significant personal-brand booster that, over time, will make you the jockey that is the one to bet on. Excellence is often subjective, thus the need to get sufficient definition. On simple tasks, where your boss is unlikely to give you an extended monologue of the task requirements (things like, "could you please organize a lunch meeting for our group to discuss a new company initiative) simply do it thoroughly . Make sure the email gets sent (spell checked) and lunch gets ordered (including the vegan lunches)."

When something is needed is as important as what is wanted—it's simple—when do you need this? If your boss tells you, "Get it to me by close of business on Thursday." Okay, is he going to work on it Thursday night?

Does he just want it in his inbox so when he shows up on Friday morning it's there waiting for him? When this happened to David, his response was, "I'm open 24/7 so 'Close of Business' means 11:59 pm to me—that's when you'll get it—at the latest." David was trying to impress with his smooth glibness and I-never-stop-working attitude; but he didn't impress his boss at all. David did, utlimately, find out when his boss really needed his stuff. The point is, find out when they want it. Find out when they really need it if you are pressed for time.

Finally, you may need to ask about a budget. We won't go into detail on that, but be prepared to ask the question if appropriate. You'll probably be asked to go prepare a budget which will eat into your already limited time to execute the task. Oh well—Do Both.

When you ultimately deliver your high-quality work product on time and on budget, remind your client or your boss that you have delivered on time and on budget. Now that we're "the boss," we like to know when someone has completed a task we've asked them to do. These tasks don't always result in something coming through my email or back across my desk, so the simple courtesy of being told it was completed closes the loop. We'll talk more about delivery notification later in this chapter.

SET GOALS

• • • • •

If you don't know where you are going,
you might wind up someplace else.

—YOGI BERRA

A critical part of your "system" should include the regular setting of goals for yourself. We know that this concept is not specifically about "delivery," but goal setting fits into the overall phylum of delivery. If goal setting is not something you have been doing already for years, you will be amazed at the power of merely setting goals for yourself and monitoring your progress towards these goals on a regular basis. Setting your own goals and follow-ing them with discipline is the difference between bouncing through life, catering to everyone else's agenda (because believe us they have one), versus carving your path through life in the direction you want to go.

We have many friends and family members that smirk at the concept of setting goals. It somehow seems too serious and formal for them—somehow taking life too seriously rather than just living, man. Well, that may be, but we only get one life, so our thinking is you may as well make the most of it. Goals are a critical part of this.

One thing that a lot of people don't realize is that goals are not all about your professional success or personal achievements. They can be (and should be) targeted towards your personal life as well as your contributions to the community and/or society overall. Whatever you want out of life—and hopefully that is more than just professional achievements—set goals and work towards them.

One of the great powers of your goals is that they will help you establish and prioritize your weekly and daily activities. As you look at your "to do" list each day, you will want to prioritize the tasks that are most important to you—meaning they are the ones that move you closer to achieving your goals. Without your own goals, your "to do" list will be filled with items that are only helping other people achieve their goals.

Now keep in mind that there are lots of types of goals: short-term, long-term, professional, personal, "bucket list" goals of what you want to do before you die, athletic goals and so on. Common ones related to your professional success should include: overall career goals, long term financial goals, five-year goals, annual goals, quarterly goals, and monthly goals.

Simon is pretty clear about this. "I always like to mix my personal and business goals as two parts of each list. Each month, I have monthly business and monthly personal goals. This is my own system for reminding me to maintain an appropriate work/life balance, and recognize that meeting my personal goals are as important if not more important than my business goals. For example, yesterday was Tuesday—normally a solid work day for me. Well, this week I chose to blow off most of the day with my kids at the zoo. Now, unfortunately, I can't afford to do that every Tuesday, or even most workdays. And I could be riddled with guilt about it today, except for the fact that I know it helped me achieve some important personal goals I have set for this month to enjoy some summer days with my kids, and to do more to 'live in the moment' when I can and while they are still young. Besides, the zoo is much less crowded on Tuesday!"

There is a certain inner peace that comes from knowing at the end of the day or week or month or year, that you completed some important tasks—personal or professional—and made progress towards some important goals. What better way could you have possibly spent your time?

So, how to get started? Invest some time over the next couple of weeks to take a first cut at establishing your set of short-term and long-term goals over the next five years, one year, quarter, and month. This sounds overwhelming, but it shouldn't take you more than a couple hours total. Keep each list relatively short—no more than ten to fifteen items. Fewer is better. Better to have a few goals that you actually achieve than a hundred that you never make progress towards. There are no right or wrong answers here, no one else needs to see them, and you can change these over time, so relax and enjoy the process.

Once you have these established, then it is merely a daily exercise (less than fifteen minutes) to check your monthly goals for that month and see which, if any, of those monthly goals you can make progress towards that day. This can also help you prioritize your daily task list in an interesting way.

At the end of the month, review your progress for the last month and set the goals for the next month. This process will become second nature after a while, and you will have a better idea of how much you can accomplish each month. Similarly, follow the same review and goal-setting process after each quarter and at the end of the year. Each year it is also appropriate to revisit the five-year and overall career goals.

Sound like a plan? Go for it! It's not hokey, or too "serious" for you. It's important, you deserve it, and you will not regret it!

HAVE A SYSTEM

· · · · ·

> *"Things which matter most must never be*
> *at the mercy of things that matter least."*
> —JOHANN WOLFGANG VON GOETHE

One of the things that has always fascinated us about the business world is that everyone seems to have their own system for managing (or in many cases, not managing) the details of their jobs and personal affairs. Look around at your next meeting—some people are taking notes on a regular pad of paper, some on some sort of Day Planner or Franklin Planner, some on their iPad, some on a PC, some not taking notes at all, some scribbling on the meeting agenda that was handed out. What is everyone going to do with their notes and action items when they leave the meeting?

Walk the halls of your office and pay close attention to how people's offices are furnished and organized. What do you see? What do you perceive about the people in those offices based on the appearance of their office? Are there files and papers and soda cans and sticky notes on every surface including the ceiling? Or is the desk surface clear of clutter, papers in neat stacks or better yet, in organized folder trays or tucked away in labeled folders? Which one of these people do you think your boss would want to trust with an important document that can't be lost? Which person is the boss most likely to stop at to chat with and introduce you to a visiting client? As you walk the halls, look at the work spaces through your boss's eyes and think about the perception you want him or her to have when they walk by your office.

Getting yourself organized and making your system highly effective is not easy to master. We're talking about how you handle all the little things— not just the notes you take when you attend a meeting, but how you plan your day, how you prioritize your tasks, how you take notes when you receive a phone call, where you put the thoughts you have about a new marketing initiative that you want to discuss at next month's staff meeting, how you handle the random client request to remind them next week about that invoice, where you put the business cards you receive at a trade conference for quick retrieval when you need them. Your files can be your best friend or your worst enemy depending on how you manage them.

Typically no one will be instructing you or coaching you about how to handle all of this stuff. But your ability to prioritize your day, to keep track of everything, to be the one that does not lose the notes, and that does not let important balls drop, will be critical to the building of the brand you want to cultivate within your company as someone on whom others can rely.

So have a system. It doesn't matter exactly what it is, and it may evolve over time just as technologies change and your personal needs will change. As long as it works for you—and you will know when it is working and when it isn't—that's all that matters.

The Franklin Planner system is one that has worked extremely well for Simon. This is just one example of the type of system that can be extremely helpful in planning your days, organizing your affairs, keeping track of all the important details in your life, and helping you to manage your time in alignment with your goals. There are other systems out there too. Shop around and see what makes sense for you. If you are like us, you will find that an unexpected benefit of organizing your work life better is that you will also be better equipped for organizing your home life and closer to achieving that elusive work/life balance as well.

David has a colleague who prints out four weeks-worth of Microsoft Outlook calendar pages—one page per week. She uses these pages to both organize her day and keep track of what she is working on. She has a national job, travels a lot and simply finds this to suit her needs. She sends a biweekly email to her boss describing what she has accomplished the previous two weeks and what she is planning to do the next two weeks. This email gets filed in an Outlook mail folder so she has a record of what she's done. While this seems a bit convoluted to David, because we're sure there are probably tools within Outlook that would make this approach more automated, she's organized. She gets a lot of stuff done, almost always answers her phone when David calls her, and seems able to make time to meet with staff to help them and mentor them. Her system works great for her.

There are several books out there that specialize on this topic. Read a couple of them and extract the nuggets that are going to make a difference for you. Talk to others who are really well organized to find out how they organize their work lives. Get a system that works for you.

DO THE HARD THINGS

• • • • •

"The toughest competitors know how to be comfortable being uncomfortable."

—LOU PINIELLA

The bravest souls do the things that everything in their body is telling them not to do. The bravest marines move toward the enemy; the bravest firefighters head into the fire; the toughest quarterbacks stand in the pocket and take the hit. You, dear business colleague, are not fighting a life-or-death situation. You are just doing business stuff. Yet, many times, the "stuff" you are doing makes you ridiculously uncomfortable.

What are some of these hard, uncomfortable things? It could be taking an overseas assignment (in some countries, these gigs are fun—in others, not so much). It could be leading a new product launch. It could be supervising someone who used to be your supervisor or mentor. It could be working with notoriously difficult people. It could be any number of things; you can fill in the blank because there are a lot of things that, if you were asked to do, would make you uncomfortable.

"There's no way I can do that," David told the CEO of his company who had just asked him to take an assignment working out of a client's office about forty miles from his home, with a cross-town drive thrown in for good measure. "Do it for six months—that's all you have to do," was what the boss said.

David took the assignment, got up every morning at 4:45 a.m. and drove across Los Angeles (the 110 through downtown if you must know) to El Segundo—every morning. "I got to the office at 6:30 a.m. because I wanted to be there before the client arrived at 6:45 a.m. I knew that he wanted to see me sitting in my office cranking away when he walked in. I stayed every day until at least 4:00, many days 5:00 p.m. or later, and then drove ninety minutes home through the worst traffic of the day. I thought I was only going to do this for six months, but I didn't realize that I had an 'indeterminate sentence' and ended up staying for seven years. It turned out to be the most significant work that I have done for any client in my career and will serve as the technical highlight of what I was able to achieve as an engineer. It was worth it—but I did not know that when I started. It was hard, it was uncomfortable, and it was, for me, career-making."

You will face many choices in your career. Some will only be uncomfortable while some will add inconvenience and difficulty in addition to discomfort. Do them. Take the challenge. Test yourself, stretch yourself—learn to be comfortable being uncomfortable.

Engineers are known to be introverts. Most of us are, in fact, introverts. David had a brief conversation with someone sitting next to him on an airplane the other day who said she was shocked that he is an engineer. So he asked her, "Do you know how you can tell an extroverted engineer from an introverted engineer? The extrovert stares at your shoes when he is talking with you instead of staring at his own." We even have our own engineering humor about our aversion to interpersonal interaction. Sadly, most of us are too shy to share this very funny joke with others.

We have worked over the years with different groups of account managers who are engineers and scientists and even the extroverts sometimes struggle in dealing with clients. They are fine having technical conversations, but they struggle with normal, "How do ya like the weather today?" types of conversations. They fear that they won't know what to say or that their hobby building cathode ray tubes will not be of interest to their client. (It probably won't be very interesting, sorry.) They fear that setting up sales meetings with clients will be unprofessional and that they will come across as too "salesy." They are afraid that the client may say "no." They don't know what to talk about with the client. They have a myriad of excuses, but the real reason is that it makes them uncomfortable.

This is an area where these engineers have to learn how to be comfortable being uncomfortable. How do they do that? Here are some steps:

- Go to a client meeting with someone who is comfortable talking with clients and observe what they do and say. (Heads up: you will need to do this more than once.)
- Ask your client about their hobbies or interests. Ask them where they travel, what they like to do on weekends, etc. And pull your head out of the latest Engineering Journal and read *Time* Magazine, *Popular* Mechanics, *National Geographic* or the daily newspaper so you have some current events that you can talk about that don't involve politics or religion. Have a list of a dozen or so things that you wouldn't mind being asked about.
- Try this out with a neighbor or friend or another work colleague who stares at her own shoes.
- Practice, Practice, Practice!
- Go for it with a client. If you fail it is not the end of the world. Get back up on the horse and try it again until you become comfortable being uncomfortable.

The first time David made a technical presentation to a client, he bombed. "The rest of my team let me know it in a pretty mean way. We got back in the car to go back to the office and they were mocking me the whole way back, repeating the dumb things I had said and laughing uproariously."

"Shortly after that, I made a presentation at a technical conference. This was a very big deal, especially for someone at my career stage. A Vice President from my company with whom I was friendly (one of the bosses who used to take me to lunch at Hutch's BBQ because I was there, in the office, available. Hint.) attended the presentation and came up to me immediately after the session ended and told me that I had done a poor job. I had. I hadn't done a good job preparing and practicing. I was winging it. I hadn't been told to prepare and practice. I was on my own, and I had a yard-sale crash."

David worked to get better and did—with practice and help from others. You can learn to be comfortable being uncomfortable. When you do, you will see clear returns for your company, your clients, and your career.

"I had a client with whom we were pursuing new work who was rightfully angry with the boorish behavior of one of our engineers. As a result, the client had black-balled" us; we would not be able to submit a proposal on any new job. My team and I were well-acquainted with the situation and felt that we had one of the best people in the area to undertake this new assignment. All things being equal, we would be tough to beat. But all things were not equal. I phoned the client and asked him if we could meet to personally apologize for the bad behavior of the soon-to-be-former-employee. I then asked if I could introduce him to the key staff member who would execute this new project if we would be allowed to compete. The client saw through the obvious strategy and agreed to a meeting in the late afternoon."

"The morning of the meeting, the key staff member walked into my office and told me he couldn't go to the meeting because his front tooth had been knocked out the previous evening and he had a dental appointment to put the tooth back in that afternoon at the same time as our client meeting. 'You're going to the client meeting. I don't care about your tooth.' He was mightily embarrassed and very uncomfortable looking like an extra from the set of *Deliverance*. I told him to keep his mouth shut and only speak if he had to. He really looked bad without that tooth—really bad.

"We went to the meeting, I apologized to the client (that isn't all that easy to do), introduced our key staff member, and thought that would be the end of it. The client started asking my colleague some questions. He had to answer them. So, he started by telling the client that he lost his tooth but came to this meeting anyway because this was an important project with an important client (yada, yada, yada). The client got a good laugh at my colleague with the missing tooth, and we ended up getting the job." Sometimes doing the hard things results in you getting to take a victory lap.

LEARN TO SELL

• • • • •

*Salesmanship is limitless. Our very living is selling.
We are all salespeople.*

—JAMES CASH PENNEY

Everybody sells stuff every day. You may not realize that you have some innate sales skills. You do. Selling is (and we know that you know this) a massively significant part of both your personal life and your work life.

You have to be both curious and resilient to sell. Curiosity is necessary to help you understand both what you are selling and the person or persons to whom you are selling. Resiliency is necessary because you, operating in sales-mode, are going to hear the word "no" quite frequently. Is selling hard to do? Yes, for some people. Is there anyone out there who likes to hear the word "no?" Nope. You have to learn how to sell stuff to effectively evolve into a leader and thrive within your organization.

Let's, hypothetically, consider your weekend planning process. It's summertime and there are a lot of options. You have to please everybody in your family of four, and yet you know for certain that pleasing everyone will be difficult if not impossible. You want to see the new Spiderman movie. Your spouse wants to go to the wine bar with friends and without the kids. The kids want to hit the pool and scream like chimpanzees who haven't been fed for three days. You have to put on your cape and become a selling Superhero or the weekend is headed to a flameout of all-around disappointment.

Often, you don't even realize that you are in a selling situation and that you are selling something to someone else. David was asked to interview a person who was retiring from a prestigious public sector job and wanted to try his hand in the private sector. "I flew fifteen hundred miles and drove two hundred more to meet this high-ranking, soon-to-retire public official in a restaurant of his choosing. I wanted to get to know this guy so I asked him a few questions about himself. He did a lot of talking—things he liked doing, interesting things he had done in his thirty years of public service, his family, his home, hunting, fishing—the full range of activities that someone who did not grow up in a big city might have an interest in. As he was blathering on about deer hunting or duck blinds (it was one of the two), he suddenly stopped and looked me in the eye and said, "I don't want to sell ... . I don't like selling, I can't sell, I won't sell anything, selling makes me nervous, I don't like salespeople, salespeople seem so pushy, I can be successful without selling, will you team me up with a salesperson, will that person be pushy ... .' It went on for at least another full, long minute. It was a full-blown stream of consciousness about the act of selling. I interrupted my new friend mid-sentence and told him he had made his point. 'You,' I told him, 'have successfully sold me that you don't feel comfortable selling.'"

You'd better learn to sell if you plan to have a successful career. You'll be selling your ideas, your work products, your proposals, and your value to the organization. You'll be selling your children on doing their homework or on going to bed at a certain time. You'll be selling your spouse or partner on what to have for dinner or what movie you'd like to see. And this is straight from the Department of Redundancy Dept—you need to learn to sell.

You don't need to learn to sell like a used-car salesperson (apologies to the fine men and women who comprise this sub-segment of our society). No one likes high pressure tactics—or any other types of overt sales tactics for that matter. Professional salespeople learn specific tactics that will entice you to buy. Smart marketing people have figured out ways to push you towards purchases of cars, shoes, clothes, personal care products, cell phones, cell phone service contracts, outdoor awnings and "pain-free" catheters (we simply can't imagine). "Send away for your free book." "While supplies last." "One day only." These are psychological devices that poke at your brain and tell you to buy. And when you give in to those neurons in your brain and make the purchase, you ask yourself, "Why did I do this?" That's the last thing you want anyone asking of you.

You need to sell value, the value in your product or service offering or the value in doing homework. High pressure tactics will turn off your sales target. Developing a value proposition that is meaningful to the sales target will grab their attention. You can tell your pre-teen son or daughter that a good night's sleep will help them in their youth soccer game the next day. You can tell your boss that you are adding value on the project by buying your client lunch at Chez Expensivo. You can negotiate with your significant other about the movie you will see on Friday night—the rom com this Friday and Spiderman next week.

Selling value means that you often have to do what's right for others, for your client, for your family or friends. It means you often don't get all that you want, but you help the other party get what they need. In the movie *Miracle on 34th Street*, Santa Claus is working at Macy's and a child asks him for a specific toy. Santa leans over to the child's mother and tells her that they don't carry that toy at Macy's, but she can purchase it at Gimbel's, a department store that is Macy's fiercest rival. That's selling value. Mom will likely have even more loyalty to Macy's for steering her in the right direction.

Finally, be prepared at all times with your own "elevator speech" about your value in the company or some new idea you'd like to share with your boss. The term "elevator speech" is well known—it refers to the amount of time you have to make a pitch as the elevator moves you and the person to whom you are talking between floors—typically fifteen to thirty seconds. If you can't convey an idea quickly and concisely, including a quick hint at the benefits of your idea, then you'll likely have a problem selling it to the people who really need to hear about it.

As for my friend who enjoyed backwoods activities but didn't want to sell—he lasted about eighteen months with our firm before he decided to call it quits and spend more time with his fishing gear. You have to be able to sell to be a conqueror in working America.

MANAGE RISKS

• • • • •

Trust—but Verify

—RONALD REAGAN

Risk management should definitely be part of your system. Project delivery is fraught with risks centered around schedule, quality, and budget. You, as the project deliverer, must consider what risks you *may* encounter and then develop mitigation measures to address these risks where you can. Most of these risks can be controlled or mitigated at some level; some are easier to control than others

The ones you can control are your risks—anything that centers on you doing stuff better or smarter. Did you leave enough time for yourself to accomplish the project elements for which you have responsibility? Did you ask enough questions? Did you actually check that someone got something done or did you just take them at their word? When negotiating a Strategic Arms Limitation Treaty with the USSR, President Ronald Reagan told the Russians that he totally trusted them but that he'd have to verify that they actually upheld their end of a bargain to dismantle nuclear weapons. We're pretty sure the term in Russian is *Doveryay, no proveryay.* Trust, but verify. We don't think, however, that President Reagan spoke any Russian.

Think about what you are doing, about things that could throw you off track, and ways to manage those things. That's called Risk Management.

Here's another one of our "colleague" stories—and by the way, these are all true with the exception that the names have been changed so we don't get sued by anyone. A colleague named Kent had a propensity for doing things at the last minute. You would get the phone call that he needed your help at 5:00 p.m. when he had something due the next morning at 10:00 a.m. It was how he lived his life. Everything he did was at the last minute. So if we were doing a risk analysis on a project that required Kent's input, we'd put him at the top of his Risk Register and probably give him a fake due date and time knowing that he'd blow it and be "late"—in his mind, but just on time in ours.

There are always signs with people like this. This was how we knew Kent was incurable. The first time David traveled with Kent to work on a project, he didn't see Kent in the boarding area for our flight. He didn't see him get on the plane. "I called him and he told me that he had arrived fifteen minutes before the scheduled departure time for this 'on-time flight,' and was just boarding the flight. He thought he was 'on time,' because he had minutes to spare. This continued every time we travelled together, so I didn't call him and just assumed he was on the flight. And then … one day, he wasn't. What happened Kent? He just cut it a little too close. He parked his car, ran into the airport to go through security, and realized that he didn't have his wallet with him. Panicking, he called his secretary to ask where he'd left his wallet (not surprisingly, she was unaware of this situation and did not know where he had misplaced his wallet.) Getting no help from his secretary who was now sobbing because he had screamed at her and berated her over the phone, he rushed back to his parked car on level 2, row J (where everyone in the company always parked for some odd reason), and found his big, fat, brimming-with-receipts wallet (another foible—why don't you take the receipts out and just dump them on your desk so your wallet isn't so fat?). He grabbed the offending wallet, which, luckily for him had not been pilfered from his vehicle where he had left it in plain sight. He rushed back into the terminal, got through security, and missed the flight. Hey Kent, Risk Management requires that you leave enough time to get through security as well as for any unforeseen stupid stuff like leaving your wallet on the dashboard of your car."

Look at what others are doing and learn from them. Figure out where they have had issues and how they resolved them so that you don't have the same issue and don't have to climb the same learning curve. One of David's family members needed hip replacement surgery. She picked a surgeon, and David asked her how she selected this surgeon. Did this surgeon have some interesting new technique or did they have more positive outcomes with their patients and where was this data published? Were they the team doctor for the Dodgers or the Rams? Did they have the biggest patient list or did they have a lot of celebrity patients? Were they a family friend or a friend of a friend? Nope. None of the above. This family member very smartly surveyed people in her very large circle of friends to see who had undergone a joint replacement and how well things had gone. Her friends who had used the surgeon that she selected had had zero problems with their recovery. Others had had issues with their surgeons. This is the "learn from others" aspect of managing risks. Quite often, if a solution works for a lot of people, it will work for you as well.

BE A LIFE-LONG LEARNER

• • • • •

"Anyone who stops learning is old, whether at twenty or eighty. Anyone who keeps learning stays young. The greatest thing in life is to keep your mind young."

—HENRY FORD

Recently, David downloaded the Starbucks mobile ordering app—for research purposes of course. He ordered, grudgingly liked the simplicity, walked his smug self up to the little mobile order counter, and waited for his beverage. "I felt so self-congratulatory in that moment, looking at all of the poor sad souls waiting in line, looking at their watches, time ticking, deadlines looming, and here I was, master of technology, time, and cappuccinos. I considered stopping my work on this book to make time for my sure-to-be bestseller oldsplaining technology to AARP members. Alas and alack, my coffee never came out. As people came and went, I became more and more incensed. After some protest, the barista kindly explained that I had ordered from the location down the street. Then she made me a fresh drink for no charge and sent me on my way because that's the kind of compassion you should show for doddering grandfatherly types. I decided to take out my frustrations on the app itself and moved it into the "food" folder where it won't stare at me when I open my lock screen."

Technology has changed, and continues to change, the business world. Let us simply say, for those of you born in the personal computer age, that what a desk looked like when Carter and Reagan occupied the Oval Office and what it looks like today are obviously very different. To start with, there probably wasn't a computer on it. Business used to be transacted by interoffice memos sent to the mail room and redistributed. You sent letters out that were delivered by snail mail. The advent of FedEx and fax machines were game-changing technological marvels.

Think of all the large and small businesses that exist today to serve business needs that were unimagined when your parents dropped their kids off at school in the family station wagon (electric car manufacturers, cloud computing, and social media optimization services are a couple examples that come to mind). Those of us born in the baby-boom years have had to be continuous learners during this time. (It wasn't easy learning how to use that fax machine. Then came email ... .) We had to, just to survive in the business environment. We're not even talking about switching companies or even industries. Do you think this pace of change is going to slow down? Don't bet on it.

Now let's set the bar a bit higher than surviving through the day. Think of all the career opportunities that get created every time there is an evolution in the way we do business. Take social media for example. In the last decade, this has evolved from a fringe form of entertainment for a few techie geeks to a central element of many large companies' customer relations and communications strategies. People now make entire careers out of designing and implementing social media strategies for customer-facing corporations. Opportunity nearly literally created out of thin air. Major evolutionary changes are more than just something to survive; they can be the source of great opportunity if you know where to look and you have the healthy attitude to look at the change with the right set of lenses.

You know where this conversation is going. You have a few options as the trains of change come rolling through. You can either turn your back, ignore the changes, and hope that they don't come fast enough to run you over before you step off the track. You can rely on others to do the learning—stepping aside while others get on the train and learn for you and hope you aren't ever "called on" to know very much about the new area while you remain in a state of dependence indefinitely. Or you can be the life-long learner, keeping your antennae out for changes early and often, taking the time you need to study and learn and adapt, effectively building up your speed so you can jump on the train—instead of getting run over—and thrive in the ever-changing world that we live in. All aboard!

About fifteen years into his career as an engineer in the utility industry, Simon made an internal switch to a newly formed group in the company that was focused on delivering management consulting services to these same utility clients. Rather than performing engineering services such as planning and designing and constructing utility infrastructure, his role in this new group was to consult with senior management of these utilities to optimize their business performance and the management of their infrastructure assets. This involved a whole new set of skills and knowledge sets covering many non-engineering topics such as organizational change, business process, data management, IT integration strategies, and performance management. "I still thought of myself as pretty young and versatile, but this was still a pretty big change for me and I was proud of my abilities to adapt to what I thought was a more promising, higher margin area of the business that presented more long-term opportunity.

"While this was a fairly significant change for me at the time, it was nothing compared to the leader of the new group who hired me. Here was a guy in his early 60s who came out of the Hydropower division of the company—he clearly got his start in the slide rule era. To confirm this, he had the girth and comb-over that identified him as a card-carrying member of the old-boy network. Yet, here he was in charge of the new strategic thrust area for the company—hiring a bunch of IT, business process, and data management guys.

"I still remember the first sales call I went on with him. We were meeting with the General Manager and the Chief Information Officer of a large utility. The conversation quickly turned to the ongoing challenges the utility had with effectively capturing, managing, and acting on data related to their buried infrastructure. For the next ten minutes, our group leader (the old guy) dove into the details of the utility's IT architecture and data platforms, exploring the details of their geographic information systems, their maintenance management systems, and their financial system—with occasional nods to the General Manager to explain in more layman's terms the business significance of these IT nuances. It was an impressive show."

Mr. Combover had mastered the specialized lingo of the IT world, been able to acquire a nice bag of new knowledge and stories to support his positions, and was now able to truly thrive in this new market space that had to be almost as foreign to him as it was to me. Impressivo! He had not just built a team and watched while they hopped on and rode the train of progress and opportunity. He had done his homework and forced himself to learn this new field to the point where he could sell it better than anyone. He had truly embraced the model of a life-long learner, demonstrating a supreme ability to adapt to changes in the business world, and he was on the front of the train yelling and screaming for it to go faster and harder into the future.

Being a life-long learner can take many forms. You don't need to be making major career changes or leading new operating divisions to justify a need for continuous learning. There is always more to learn about nearly every job that exists. Aside from learning specific technical topics that might closely relate to your current job, you can always benefit by taking a course, attending a seminar, or picking up a book on various general topics. Some of our favorites include:

- Leadership
- Communications
- Management
- Coaching
- Negotiation
- Sales
- Public Speaking
- Business Optimization
- Performance Management

Ask your boss and your peers whether they have read any good business books lately. We guarantee that your CEO has read something lately that you might find interesting. Try reading at least one new business book each quarter and attending at least one seminar or training class each year. Force yourself to share what you learn with your peers or your staff—it will drive you to get more out of these learning opportunities and enable you to spread the wealth of knowledge to others.

Do you hear any trains coming?

CAN YOU HEAR ME NOW?

• • • • •

"If a tree falls in the forest and no one is around to hear it, does it make a sound?"

—GEORGE BERKELEY

You are doing good work. Your team is doing great work. Everything is on schedule. Everything is on budget. Victory is in sight. Does anyone know this. Are you keeping your boss or your client (or both) informed of your fantastic efforts? Unless you have established a continuous Vulcan mind meld with your boss or your client, or they are physically looking over your shoulder every day, you can be certain that they don't, in fact, have any idea how you are progressing on your project. There are a few things you can do to demonstrate that the magical outputs of your team's work efforts are going to make your client say, "WOW!"

This is not about taking credit. This is about delivery and putting a metaphorical ribbon and bow on your package. People are busy. If you don't tell them, they won't know. What are some good ways to tell them? You can start with talking to them periodically. Once a week, once a day, once a month—the frequency depends on the length of your schedule but the key point is that you tell them what you've been doing, what you are planning to do, and how you are doing with respect to schedule and budget. I realize that telephone conversations went out of vogue sometime between the Red Sox ending their World Series drought and the Cubs ending their even longer Worlds Series drought. Perhaps you can do a weekly report or an email, or even a text because we know you have built up sufficient endurance in your thumbs to do so. Whatever it is, you need to communicate as your project progresses.

The second aspect of communication is that you need to let people know you heard their message when they message you. When you get a voice mail or an email or a text asking you about some aspect of your work, you need to respond to that message and either provide a direct response to the person asking the question or let them know when you will get back to them. If they don't hear from you, they will assume that you did not hear the tree falling in the forest!

Finally, when you deliver your final product, you need to have face-to-face conversation with your client or your boss and let them know what you are delivering. Sometimes going face-to-face is difficult when you and your client are in different time zones, different area codes, or even different countries. If you can't go face-to-face, then you should call them and talk to them. Very old-fashioned, I know, but they'll be impressed with your abilities to have a phone conversation with them. What should you tell them? Tell them what they are getting. Keep it short: two or three sentences to describe what you are delivering. Talk with them about next steps. Remind them of activities that they will undertake to review your work product. Thank them for the opportunity. Ask them what additional projects you can do for them. In short, let them know you have delivered what they have requested and that you would love to continue to work with them. That way, they'll know!

You at the Helm—Last Looks

You are the captain of your own ship. You can steer your career destiny to the ports that you desire. How do you do this? You evolve into a prepared, organized, tough, smart, communicative leader. Yes, all of those things and probably a few more will be part of your leadership ethos. As you evolve and as you engage as a leader, you'll find the place where Us makes the most sense for you, your team, your bosses, your clients, and even Mr. Combover. Now, you are beginning to *thrive.*

FIVE

The Future You

Leadership—How YOU Make US Better

L EADERSHIP IS THE ASPIRATIONAL GOAL OF THE CLIMB. LEADERSHIP IS your opportunity to fix all the stuff that previous bosses have done. You may find yourself thinking, "If I ever get to be the boss there is no way I'm going to do this dumb stuff." When you are the leader, you are going to get your opportunity to be the dumb-stuff-fixer.

You may lead a group, be a Subject Matter Expert and lead other SMEs in your organization, or have the opportunity to lead your clients. Your opportunity may come at work, in a professional organization, at church, in your family, or at the neighborhood pickleball tournament. You should take every opportunity to work at your leadership skills and become a better leader. Whatever form your leadership opportunity takes and wherever the opportunity presents itself, you should be ready because great leadership will propel you up the ladder faster than anything else you can do.

There are many great books on leadership, and this is certainly not one of them. We don't intend to give you the details and the examples that other books so ably provide. We do, through this chapter, intend to give you some ideas and thoughts on leadership in the context of your career arc. It's just food for thought. If you are looking for a book on leadership, pick up anything written by Doris Kearns Goodwin about Presidents Abraham Lincoln, Teddy Roosevelt, Franklin Roosevelt, or Lyndon Johnson. These will give you real examples of great people who understood leadership in uneasy times.

If you're doing things right, you get to become "the boss" (you get to be the Them that's creating the "us"). We want to give you some of our insights into leadership, starting with "remember where you came from." There are many who want to be You, who aspire to your position, and who want to learn from You. A fair dose of humility will be appreciated by all. David recalls the first time he was given a major promotion, he called his wife to let her know. "That's nice honey," she said, "I've got to go now and take care of four little kids." She told David—like a boss! Let's look at some aspects of Leadership that don't necessarily involve changing diapers.

INSPIRE

• • • • •

> *"Perpetual optimism is a force multiplier."*
> —GENERAL COLIN POWELL

As a leader, how do you get people to do what you need them to do? Do they do what they need to do because they fear you? Do you promise rewards for their acceptable job performance? Do you say, "Just do this and you can _____ (fill in the blank with such things as "keep your job," " take your vacation days," "get a bonus," etc.). You know in your heart that this doesn't work for you. You don't want to work for someone who does this. They aren't leaders: they are cattle rustlers.

Threats and promises don't work. Leadership is about inspiration. We are NOT going to talk about how one inspires, rather, we are simply going to encourage you to be inspirational in three ways.

First, be a storyteller. People simply relate to stories, and they really relate to real stories. (How's that for alliteration?) David tells the story of his toothless colleague and the mad client (see *Do the Hard Things*) frequently to make a point about doing the hard things. Simon tells stories about colleagues who have inspired him. We both tell stories from books we have read including biographical tidbits, leadership lessons, and amazing accomplishments. (Did you know that Abraham Lincoln was largely self-taught because his father could not afford to send him to school—hat tip to Doris Kearns Goodwin.)

David says, "I like to quote movie lines, and I often show clips from movies that I think will be educational and memorable. (I like a three minute segment from the movie *Tommy Boy* as an example of how NOT to sell.) I have a few favorite Shakespeare quotes that I use frequently—if nothing else, they get people to listen very carefully to what I am saying. AND, I'm really passionate when I relay these stories or quotes because they all mean something to me or they have actually happened to me. I don't tell a story just for the sake of being funny or entertaining. I'm always trying to make a point." Have a bag of stories you can tell to illustrate points you want to make. Learn to tell your stories in an interesting and memorable way.

Secondly, understand that people will learn as much, maybe more, from failures as they do from successes. David says, "I don't always talk about successes. I'm a fallible human being just like the next person—sometimes I blow it. I've learned a lot from my mistakes, and I want my pain to be your gain. Here's an example. I went and visited a client who happened to be a friend —well, our wives are close friends and, as a result, we also are friends. I tell the story of going into the meeting unprepared. I had spent a minimal amount of time putting together two topics to discuss with my friend/client. We talked about our kids, we talked about the Dodgers, and then I introduced my first technical idea. Then my friend/client asked me a question that I couldn't answer and that was pretty much it. We went back to rehashing our Dodgers discussion. With a little bit of forethought and one phone call, I could have come up with an answer to this question and probably most any other question he may have asked. I didn't do my homework and I wasted a meeting. People get it when I share this with them. If I was perfect, no one should listen to me—people know that no one is perfect." The ability to take shots at yourself while delivering the message is useful in developing your credibility, driving home your point, inspiring others to rise above their fears and inconsistencies, and doing the things you need them to do.

Finally, BE PASSIONATE. Yes, we intended to scream that at you. If you don't believe in what you are saying, DO NOT SAY IT (scream also intentional here). We have witnessed colleagues who are passionate about their area of expertise, make the impossible sale to the client, convince executive management to make investments, and get their teams to accomplish goals that they had not thought possible. These colleagues combine their expertise in their subject matter with their passion for their subject matter—and that is a powerful combination. Say it like you believe it. Say it like you know it to be absolutely true.

David was asked to give a forty-five-minute presentation on client service to a group of mid-level managers. He was emphatic. "This is one of MY topics—I know about client service in our markets. The morning of the presentation I got sick—the kind of sick that makes you not want to wander too far from a 'facility.' I was in agony, but I had made a commitment, and as long as I was *compos mentis,* I would meet that commitment. I decided to give it everything I had. I walked into the room, drew a big two-by-two matrix on a white board that would have made a Harvard Business School professor proud, and started to talk and draw at the same time. I have no idea what I said, and I really had to bolt out of the room right after I finished—but several people came up to me later and complimented me on my mastery of the topic and especially my passion for the topic.

When you have passion, it can overcome illness, it can overcome fear of speaking, it can overcome mistakes you might make when you are speaking—it can make your subject matter, your vision, come alive and it can turn others into believers.

And that is what inspirational leaders do!

Messaging

· · · · ·

"If you want a love message to be heard,
it has to be sent out. To keep a lamp burning,
we have to keep putting oil on it."

—Mother Teresa

Leaders set the tone and provide guidance and goals through messaging. Clear messages are the best way for a leader to convey what they expect from their team. Okay, we know you know this. There are two very notable things about Mother Teresa: first was how she delivered her message and the second, and possibly more important, was the consistency between her message and her life.

Mother Teresa's message was consistent and persistent and, as a leader, she got to be insistent. What does this mean? A consistent message is just that, consistent. We want our team to deliver work products to our clients on time. To be consistent, we talk about timely delivery as one of our top priorities. Every talk that one of us gives about customer service, we talk about timely delivery. That's a consistent message. Consistent messages should be clear and unambiguous. In fact, all messages should be clear and unambiguous. Consistency drives home the point you want to make and ultimately plants that point in the heads of those you wish to influence.

A persistent message means that you talk about my consistent message over and over and over. It almost becomes a joke, but it's not, because when you're consistent, your team knows you're serious *and* passionate about it. See every interaction as an opportunity to talk about this message. Take one-on-one interactions as those opportunities as well as group presentations. If you are passionate and have a strong message for your team, deliver it in a consistent manner and be persistent; never stop.

Just a quick interjection about the second aspect of Mother Teresa's messaging. There was obvious consistency between her message of love and her actions of love. You can't lead without both. You need the words. You need the actions. Your consistent and persistent words are insufficient and meaningless unless you have both. People can always see a fraudulent leader. They are the people who demand you work late to finish a project but go home early so they can booze it up in their hot tub. They are the people who ask you to do things that they would never do themselves. That ain't leadership. That's fraud.

Finally, as a leader, you earn the right to be **insistent**. Because of Simon's position in the company, he can insist that his staff treat their clients a certain way. He almost never plays the **insistent** card, however. Instead he is persistent in his efforts to consistently try to inspire people. We think that's a better way. If you need it, "insistence" is a good tool to have in your tool box.

Consistent. Persistent. Insistent.

LISTEN

• • • • •

> *"Courage is what it takes to*
> *stand up and speak; courage is also what*
> *it takes to sit down and listen."*
>
> —WINSTON CHURCHILL

The best leaders are often fantastic listeners. But many leaders are not. Why is that? Perhaps it's the mistaken belief that leaders are "demanders." Some people think that they can demand things of others on the basis of their position in an organization, their amazing business skills, their breathtakingly expensive Ivy League education, or the fact that their daddy owns the company. Only the "daddy" thing gives them the right, and even that really shouldn't mean that they can be "demanders."

One of your goals as a leader is to get everybody "on the same page." What this really means is that you want everyone on your team working toward a common goal and doing exactly their job so that the team can produce a harmonious and congruent outcome. The only way you can do this is to let everyone have their say. Great leaders are listeners. They gather information from others, solicit opinions, and want people to question their thinking. This is one of the ways they get everyone working together.

Leaders do their information gathering, then process it, before they offer their final decisions on the toughest issues. General Eisenhower did this before ordering the D-Day invasion of France, first planned for June 5, 1944. He cancelled the first invasion date due to weather and ordered it again the next day after he had consulted with the meteorologist, other General offices, Naval Admirals, and other strategists. He made the biggest decision of his life—perhaps the most seminal decision of the 20th Century on the basis of the information gained by listening to smart people (not all of whom agreed with the June 5 or June 6 invasion date by the way).

In David's company, every presentation starts with a "safety moment." This is just a brief reminder to be safe and vigilant in some area of our lives. A reminder to wear sunscreen is a good safety moment. David had piled up three safety moments that he rotated in and out of a presentation that he gave in various branch offices on client service. He thought they were clever and cute, but he never got a response when he showed them. "Following a presentation in one of our offices, I asked a colleague I trusted what he thought of the particular 'safety moment' slide that I had shown during my presentation."

"Dumb," he said.

"Okay, how about these other two?"

"Dumb and Dumber," was his response.

Sigh. "'What about this one,' I asked showing him a safety moment slide that I thought was just so-so.'

"Yeah, that's really clever and useful," he told me.

David trashed the bad ones (one of which included a photo of one of his grandchildren and that was a tough one to drag into the trash) and inserted the one his colleague liked.

Leaders listen.

GIVE AND TAKE

• • • • •

"I early learned that it is a hard matter to convert
an individual by abusing him, and that this is more often
accomplished by giving credit for all
the praiseworthy actions performed than by
calling attention alone to all the evil done."

—BOOKER T. WASHINGTON

How many times have you sat in a meeting, said something insightful, and then, several minutes later, someone gives credit for your insightful comment to someone else? How many times have you been part of a team and done something that was absolutely critical to the team's success and the credit for your achievement goes unrecognized or worse yet, is ascribed to someone else? It's not a good feeling. The converse is true as well. It hurts to take the blame for failure when it's a team effort or a leadership problem. Leaders have to learn what it means to give and to take. They have to give credit, and they have to take responsibility.

Credit for the successful outcome of a business endeavor rarely rests on the shoulders of one individual. It truly is a team effort. As the leader, you have to give the credit to your team. If the CEO wants to give you the company's highest honor, the Order of the Almighty Dollar, or whatever the award is, that's great. You can accept it on behalf of your team. When the client calls to thank you, you can tell her that it's a team effort. Giving credit to your team and not taking credit for yourself is an essential element of leadership. It's one of the things that your team members will find inspirational. It's one of the things that will get people to follow you again and again as you undertake difficult assignments.

The converse of this is to take responsibility for failure. No one wants to do this. A quote commonly attributed to President John F. Kennedy (we used this quote earlier in the book) was actually first uttered by an Italian nobleman at the onset of the Second World War. Count Galeazzo Ciano said, "Victory has a hundred fathers and defeat is an orphan." No one wants to take credit for defeat but you, as a leader, have to stand up and take responsibility for a poor outcome. You were the team leader, and your team did not deliver. Great leaders take the slings and arrows that come with defeat to protect their team. It's another one of the things that will get people to follow you again and again.

Great military leaders understood this concept. General Eisenhower feared that D-Day would not be successful and had already prepared a note accepting responsibility for its failure. The note made it clear it was his sole responsibility. Great political leaders throughout history, like Abraham Lincoln, understood this and stood ready to take responsibility for failures. Lincoln took responsibility for military failures during the Civil War to take the heat off his generals. Great sports leaders understand this. The team leaders will take responsibility for the loss of a championship game because they understand this concept and they know that, to achieve victory the next time they have an opportunity, they need the entire team following them and working as one.

PUBLIC SPEAKING— WORSE THAN DEATH?

• • • • •

"It usually takes me more than three weeks to prepare a good impromptu speech."
—MARK TWAIN

Many people hate public speaking. Many people fear public speaking. They fear it more than death. They would rather die than stand up in front of others and say a few words or maybe more than a few words. If this is true, according to Jerry Seinfeld, people should prefer to be in the coffin rather than standing up and giving a eulogy at a funeral. If you intend to lead others and you are deathly afraid of public speaking, you'll have to change your preferences. You'll have to be the one wanting to give the eulogy. Can this be done? Of course it can, and just to reassure you, many have gone before you and overcome their very rational, sensible fear of public speaking. Let's explore how you may do this.

Practice makes perfect. That's what we were told as children, and it didn't work out so well for most of us unless you are named Yo-Yo Ma or Slash. One of us played the cello (he was awful and didn't practice) and the guitar (also awful and he *did* practice) and no amount of practice could help him overcome his God-given lack of abilities on these two instruments. Nevertheless, if you can speak, you can speak in public. If your mouth can be used to utter words and complete (or partially complete) sentences, then you can utter sentences or some fraction thereof in a public setting. You have to practice, practice, and practice some more.

You have to practice public speaking in public. Yes, in public, in front of others. That's the only way you can practice *public* speaking. You can practice the talk that you will be giving in public in your bathroom or bedroom, staring into a mirror, or staring into a wall. You can do that to get prepared to practice public speaking, and you should do that to get prepared for your public speaking engagement. You simply cannot become a better public speaker if you only speak to yourself. You have to speak to others—many others—that's what public speaking is all about.

There are many ways to do this. One way that has been shown to be very successful is Toastmasters. We're sure that there is a Toastmasters group near you. They are all over the place and they will give you ample opportunity to hone your skills. There are public speaking classes at Community Colleges that you may find to be useful. Many companies offer internal programs and public speaking opportunities. Take advantage of these. Practice, Practice, and Practice.

While you are practicing, listen to what others have to tell you. David took a public speaking course offered by a communications firm in San Francisco. As part of this course, he spoke in front of the group seven times. Each speaking opportunity was videotaped so that he could be critiqued by one of the instructors and given an assignment to get better at some aspect of his public speaking skill set during the ensuing presentation. "I was told to use my hands more and stop fiddling with my watch. I was taught how to use motion effectively. I was told to change the volume of my voice to create emphasis. I was told a lot of stuff, quite honestly, and it seemed overwhelming. I was glad that I went and put myself through the class. I had to listen to others to get better."

Similarly, you should borrow ideas from other public speakers who you think are great speakers. It's not a big deal, it's really a compliment to them. We don't mean that you should plagiarize their speech. That's not borrowing, that's theft. Rather, you should borrow aspects of their style that you think would fit your style. Ultimately, unless you are super creative, your public speaking will be a compendium of many styles that you have seen and been taught. That's okay. You can borrow multiple styles and blend them together to create your own uber-cool speaking style.

Great speakers have a message and they can frame it in a memorable way. Think about your key message and deliver it. This is part of the consistent/persistent leadership theme. Your message should be clear and backed up by facts, stories, anecdotes, and more facts.

If you believe in your message, then you should bring the thunder. Bring the level of passion that is appropriate to your message. It will be different depending on the topic and the audience. You'll know what to do. Just make sure that, where it is appropriate, you let your passion for the topic shine through.

LEADERSHIP CAN BE LEARNED

• • • • •

"Leaders aren't born, they are made. And they are made
just like anything else, through hard work.
And that's the price we'll have to pay
to achieve that goal, or any goal."
—VINCE LOMBARDI

You're always complaining that your boss doesn't do the right thing or that the company does the dumb thing. Yes, you are probably right. Great leaders learn how to do the right thing and inspire people around them with their passion, work ethic, and timely words to join them in doing the right thing. You can learn to be a great leader who does this.

The first thing in learning to be a leader is to find a leader who you would like to emulate. This could be your mentor or your mentor's mentor. It could be someone that you know through a professional organization or your church. Watch, listen, and learn. It's one of the best ways to learn about leadership. David worked for many different people from whom he learned different aspects of leadership. "One person taught me about confronting bad behavior when he hauled me into his office to very sternly tell me about my one particularly poor response to one of the administrative staff. Another taught me about organization. I learned about planning from another leader. Some of these people I was working for at the time and others were leaders in different parts of the company that I thought had their act together in specific areas."

One leader taught us about making something memorable. We were trying to deliver a particularly complicated report to a client and this leader brought our team together one afternoon and said, May 14. He just stood there smiling.

One brave soul asked, "What does that mean?"

"It means," our leader said, "that our report is due to the client on May 14." We were shocked because we didn't have much time to get things done. We spent the rest of our meeting time discussing and agreeing on how we would accomplish this herculean task in the time allotted. When we asked this leader why he did this, he said "EPA—Event Precipitated Action." When something has a hard delivery date, we just had to deliver. That was his leadership tool—EPA.

Leaders have to overcome fear, and this is something, again, that you can learn. You don't have to jump out of an airplane or walk across hot coals to be a leader, but you do have to display fearlessness in the face of a daunting task. Your team will look to you, as the leader, to be the one to display the confidence that a task can be completed. You have to be fearless and believe that you, and your team, can deliver.

Some young leaders are in situations where they are leading people who are older and more experienced. You need to remember that leadership is age agnostic. It doesn't matter how old you are and how old they are. What matters is that you display leadership skills to organize and manage your team. David had to overcome the age thing early in his career, and it was very difficult for him at first. "I struggled with the senior people on the team. I was too deferential, almost to the point that I was asking them to tell me what to do. What I didn't know was that they were fine with me leading the team. They were decent people who were at a point in their careers where they preferred to just solve complex engineering problems and let the leadership stuff be handled by others. They didn't care about my age or lack of experience. When they saw things going awry, they gave me advice, we righted the ship, and moved forward."

Age doesn't matter. Confidence, passion and willingness to take advice are key.

STAY IN TOUCH WITH THE TRENCHES

• • • • •

"Always do everything you ask of those you command."
—GEORGE S. PATTON

In 1917, Black Jack Pershing took the American Expeditionary Force to France to enter World War I. He established a headquarters at an estate called Chaumont where he required all of the generals to be located. The front lines, the trenches, were a hundred miles away. Battles raged during the day and the front-line commanders sent information back to Chaumont by motorcycle courier every evening. The generals caucused with each other, made plans, put those plans on paper, put the paper in the hands of the motorcycle couriers, who then transported them to the front-line commanders. The Chaumont-based generals then waited until the following evening when the couriers returned with news of the next day's battles, and the process started all over again.

One young general, a guy named Douglas MacArthur, decided to stay at the front lines. He didn't need a motorcycle courier. He could see for himself what was happening, make on-the-spot decisions that could be directly conveyed to the troops and then thoughtfully craft plans for the next day's battle using unfiltered data. He commanded the top-performing battalions of the American Expeditionary Force—because he had real, firsthand, front-lines knowledge of what went on in the trenches. General MacArthur knew the skill sets of his commanders and troops and was able to put them into positions where they could be successful.

The trenches are where business gets done. It's not the same as the trenches of the First World War. It is, however, the place where one can gain real-time knowledge regarding the conduct of your company's business, and the ways that your clients use your company's products and services. This is important information that you can't fully appreciate if it comes to you in a handwritten dispatch carried by a dude who rode in on a 1918 vintage Harley. You can only learn it for yourself by being there and being part of the action.

A highly placed person in our company liked to tell our team how to negotiate contracts with our clients. This individual had never, to my knowledge, successfully negotiated a contract with any of our clients. He did, however, demand that we take specific negotiation positions that we knew would never be acceptable to our clients. In one instance that is particularly memorable, this individual told us to go back to the client one more time to try and get them to change a certain paragraph in a contract, after the client had told us that if we asked for this change one more time they would cease negotiating with us and give the contract to another firm. We're proud to say that we disregarded this instruction, didn't get the change that "the man" asked us to get, got the contract. and successfully completed the work.

It's pretty clear that the reason we were directed to take these positions was that this highly placed person was completely out of touch with the trenches. This person occasionally visited clients, but rarely negotiated, had never delivered a product to a client and had certainly never sat across the desk from an angry client who was upset about service-delivery problems. The only way you can learn what it's like is to be on the front lines and learn through experience.

As one rises through the ranks, one tends to be separated from clients if one chooses to allow this to happen. It doesn't have to happen that way and it certainly doesn't have to happen to you. Clients are what make your company successful. If cash is king (or queen), clients provide the cash flow that determines ultimately whether your company stays in existence or goes the way of the Dodo bird. Understanding your clients is critical to business success—AND (why is there always an AND or a BUT?) client needs, concerns, requirements, buying behaviors, buying processes, etc. are dynamic, not static. They are always changing as the world around your clients and their organizations change. You can guess at client needs and buying behaviors. Your CEO, CFO, CTO, CXO—they can all guess at these things and they'd tell you that they are pretty good at guessing. Why guess?? Stay connected with your clients, stay connected with those on the front lines who are connected to clients.

A colleague got promoted to a mid-level line management position and asked David what he thought this new manager should "do with his clients."

David's advice was simple: "Stay close to them. Never, ever throw away your 'Little Black Book.'" Your clients—your success with your clients—is likely one of the most significant reasons you have moved up in your organization. Stay involved in product or project delivery. Maintain a detailed understanding of why your clients buy from your company and what your company can do to consistently exceed your clients' expectations.

You should also stay connected to your staff in the field and in branch offices. You know what your direct reports are doing, but do you actually know the people who report to them— and we mean "know" as in know their name, know about their families, know about their skills, know about their client relationships and know what they are doing to further the goals of your company. The best leaders we have ever seen know the capabilities of every key person. Don't guess at it; don't take second- or third-hand information about people. If you lead a big team it is your job to really know as many people as possible so you, like General MacArthur, can put people in the right spots to be successful.

Stay connected to the trenches. You'll never regret it.

BEING THERE

· · · · ·

"That sir which serves and seeks for gain,
and follows but for form, will pack when it begins
to rain, and leave thee in the storm."
—WILLIAM SHAKESPEARE

Leaders must be available in the good times and the bad. You can't really lead effectively if you spend your days in Chaumont and your team is in the trenches. Not only should you be with your team, you should be responsive to your team.

Responsiveness means that you respond—to emails, texts, and phone calls. Some day you may have some wearable device made by Apple that allows you to share your mind with your team and you won't have to use a phone or computer. We're not there yet, and the people you lead are most likely in need of information from you otherwise they wouldn't be contacting you. Respond to them. Call, text, email them back. Provide the information, reassurance, and positive energy that they require and are asking for.

One of our colleagues was well known for not responding. He always had an excuse. "I was on a plane." "I was in a meeting." "I was binge-watching *Hogan's Heroes.*" Whatever the excuse, except for binge-watching a 1970's vintage TV show, we all have the same issues. Planes, trains, automobiles, meetings and lunches with clients—we were all in the same boat. It became a joke at the executive level. Everyone liked this person, but no one could work with him. Ultimately, the person demanded a promotion which was not forthcoming and left the company. We still work with him from time-to-time and we all ironically chuckle at his horrible habit of non-responsiveness.

Get back to people. It tells them that you think they are an important part of your organization and that you will take your own precious time to help them, talk to them, and lead them.

HAVE THICK SKIN

• • • • •

Good work ain't cheap; cheap work ain't good.
—NORMAN "SAILOR JERRY" COLLINS,
PIONEER TATTOO ARTIST

Another key aspect of being an effective leader is doing your best to be a shining example of how to handle feedback and criticism from all of those you work with—your boss, your peers, and your direct reports. And not just *handle* the feedback, but actually listen to it and benefit from it. Because guess what, no matter how high up the corporate ladder you go, you will never know everything, and, yes, you're going to get it wrong sometimes and people are going to let you know. As you gain more and more experience, this may happen less often than in the beginning, but believe us it will happen.

It will help if you try to always remember the fact that you do not have a monopoly on all of the good ideas. You may think you are the expert on a topic and have the ability to think everything through on your own, but they beauty of good teams is that they are comprised of people that bring different perspectives to the table and, if properly harnessed, the team's collective brain power far exceeds any individual's capacity to develop ideas and solutions. This is not easy to remember when you are in the middle of a perfectly planned presentation to your team—trying to roll out the next world-beating corporate initiative—when a hand goes up and a comment comes out of left field that calls into question one of your key points. Ouch.

What are your choices at this point? For most of us, our first temptation is to protect our own ego. Thoughts we're familiar with: surely this person hasn't thought this through as well as I have? They have vastly less experience so surely their brainpower is vastly inferior to mine! How dare they? You will be tempted to blow off this comment and waive it away as irrelevant and perhaps give some trite response like, "Let me get through these slides and we can discuss that later." That might get you through the presentation, but you have probably not convinced anyone that the point was not a valid one, nor have you allowed for consideration of what could have been an important issue for your team to discuss.

Now ask yourself, what would a great leader do? What would a confident person do—someone with thick skin who was not wrapped up in worrying about their own ego and most concerned about arriving at the best solution for their company? Such a leader might say, "That's interesting. Tell me more about what is on your mind?" and then perhaps turn to the rest of the group, "Does anyone have any thoughts on how to address this?" With these types of comments, you have shown you value input from your team, you are open to ideas, and everyone feels involved in the process. Sure, you might have lost a little time in getting to the implementation phase of your plans, but you will likely get to a better solution in the end, as well as earning your stripes as an effective leader.

David describes a former colleague with a "response phenomenon" named after him—it's called the Ray Rule of Three. Quite simply, when presented a new concept for the first time, his response was always negative. When he was feeling particularly magnanimous, he'd say, "I have no idea what you are talking about." This response was not just for business concepts. When Ray asked a subordinate to prepare a document for him or to undertake some other task his typical response upon receiving the document for the first time was to reject it as insufficient.

Several months later, he'd hear the same concept the second time, and his response had now morphed into, "That's fascinating and really interesting, but I don't see how it applies to me or any of my clients." Often these responses were in larger group meetings and were intended by Ray to demonstrate his "critical" thinking skills. To Ray, critical thinking meant that one would criticize another person's thinking. I guess that makes sense in an apocalyptic, zero-sum-game way where there is one winner and everyone else is a loser. Ray was making sure he was, at least in his own mind, the winner.

It's not called the Ray Rule of Three for nothing because there was indeed a third response from our anti-hero. Another few months would elapse, and the same concept would be presented again. Ray would now say, "That's brilliant. Why didn't you tell me that the first time?"

There's a Ray in every crowd, in every big group meeting, in every client meeting. Sometimes they speak up and sometimes they don't. Just recognize that interesting ideas and concepts often have to be explained three times to your "Ray" before the "critical thinkers" actually get it—or admit that they get it.

When someone tells one of us, "thank you for your wonderful work and next time, could you do X and Y slightly better," we ignore this request. Why, if the work was "wonderful" should it be "better"? In this case, understand that the term "wonderful" isn't being used in the Webster's standard definition kind of way. When your work is compared to the myriad of barnyard animals who leave excrement around the barnyard, then you have got to listen. It's personal. It's very personal to have your work proclaimed to be animal excrement. So having someone call your work wonderful isn't as damaging to the ego. Both are signals for you to do better—so take them as such. If the person telling you this really didn't care about you, they'd probably say nothing—why waste your breath on someone who can't improve? They are telling you because they want you to improve. You should also recognize that most people who feel that they need to shock you into reality with their barnyard comparisons believe they can't get your attention with a "please make your wonderful work better the next time around" kind of statement. Pay attention to criticism so that you can indeed improve your skills.

You don't need constant feedback—that can be (well, actually it is) very irritating. Periodic feedback is really useful. The problem is you're likely to get it from "Ray," or the guy who has the propensity for comparing your work to animal excrement. You can still use this to get better. Have thick skin and deliver higher quality work products.

One other tangential aspect of this is how to handle things when you mess up. What—you don't ever make mistakes??!! Great, then you can skip this paragraph and move on to the next section. Oh— you actually do let a few minor errors get past you from time to time. Fair enough, you're only human after all. What should you do? Here's a complicated formula to consider:

1. Apologize—"Wow, I'm sorry I missed that"
2. Get Advice—"How can I do this better?"

When you apologize, you are doing more than admitting a mistake. You are telling the other person that you are validating their comment. You are making it harder for that person to react to you angrily. In the world of medicine, apologies from physicians accused of malpractice often act to assuage the patient and reduce the likelihood of a malpractice suit. We think that works for other areas of professional endeavor. We aren't perfect. We, on occasion, make mistakes. We should apologize when we do.

Then we should try to do better. You won't always get advice when you ask the question, "How can I do better?" It is, however, worth asking the question and if your client or boss or peers or subordinates won't tell you, ask others on your team or your friends what you can do better. Always be learning and have thick skin!

EMBRACE CHANGE ...
AND CHOOSE TO LEAD IT

• • • • •

"Change is the law of life. And those who look only to the past or present are certain to miss the future."
—JOHN F. KENNEDY

You get a new boss; a key employee is recruited by the competition; the competition releases a breakthrough product like the iPhone; the housing bubble bursts; your company gets acquired; your company decides to expand to a new continent. Change happens. Sometimes it's large, sometimes it's small. Sometimes it's intentional and part of some grand idea or design of a few big thinkers in your organization. Sometimes it's something that nobody foresaw, and nobody could control. Usually it just happens, and everyone is caught off guard at the same time. This can be a major source of confusion, stress, and frustration for you. Or, you can see it as a major source of excitement and opportunity. Rest assured that change will happen during your career, and the choice will be yours (usually) as to how to respond to the change.

There has been much written about organizational change and change management. In our increasingly fast-paced business environment, the ability of an organization to effectively handle change is becoming more and more critical in order to maintain competitiveness over the long term. The same goes for individuals. As we finish up our book, our world is addressing the coronavirus pandemic. This too, is an example of change. How will you respond to societal changes that impact your work? In David's company, the CEO, Keith, got out in front of this with emails and video conferences

157

telling people to work from home and keep themselves well; and he did this a week before it became a United States Centers for Disease Control recommendation. Keith saw the change and got out in front of it. He was leading the effort with crisp, clear directions and some cheerleading, reminding healthy people to actually keep working to continue to support our clients.

He's the CEO. That's his job—to lead in tough times. Yes, it is. Plenty of other leaders swing and miss at the curveball of change even for the most rudimentary of issues. In the 1990s, "casual Friday" became a "thing" in many companies, ours included. David worked for a regional manager who ran one of the biggest operating units in the company; a very powerful guy. "He sent out a three-page memo offering his definition of 'casual' attire. It was a joke, and he got a lot of negative feedback from a lot of people, including me. I told him, 'If you have to write a three page memo to define *casual*, then it's not casual. Just let people work this out over time and if someone wears something inappropriate, you can have a chat with them about your definition of *casual*.'" Changes in societal and corporate norms don't come from the boardroom, yet they are just as important for the leader to understand, and where possible, lead.

If you want to thrive and excel in your organization, you need to be equally or more adept at handling change than your peers. You need to be seen as someone who will "get on board" and embrace change, not as someone who is a "dinosaur" and a potential barrier to change. Notice that we said "be seen as" because there may be times when perception may not match reality. You might think the new boss is a fool and his or her new initiatives are even more foolish. You may be thinking "we tried that before and it didn't work." Be careful!

You need to be careful to manage your reputation and brand during times of change, even when you don't agree. There is nothing a new boss hates more than an old crusty employee who can't embrace change and is seen as a barrier and negative influence on the rest of the organization because they are telling everyone "we've done this before, and it didn't work." This attitude will never stop the change, but it may very well stop your paycheck!

Even better than embracing change is offering to lead the change. Put yourself in the position of your new boss. She may be giving off the impression that she is 100 percent sure of herself; she has seen this work elsewhere before and all will be fine if we just follow her. This is a good image for her to maintain, but the reality is there will always be doubt and she will always have some fear that the new initiative will be a flop and she will look foolish.

Here's where you come in. You could be the stick-in-the-mud saying we have tried this before, and it won't work. The dark clouds above your head raining on the rest of the group will increase the likelihood of her initiative failing and her looking foolish. This is a not a position you want to be in.

Think about an alternative approach. You catch your new boss alone at her desk late one afternoon and politely ask for a few minutes of her time. You start by telling her how much you care about the company and how much you want the group to succeed under her leadership. If you have some specific concerns about the new initiative, you could mention them from the standpoint of asking her advice as to how she thinks we can overcome these concerns. Then you can make it clear that she has your unflinching support to make this successful, and you can also ask her if there is anything extra you could do to help lead this change to make sure everyone is successful.

How does your new boss perceive you? Hopefully not as someone who is full of s$%*@t, but rather as someone who truly cares about the company and someone who can help her succeed in her initiative and reduce the likelihood of her failing and looking foolish. You might be just the employee she needs to solidify public opinion for her ideas.

It's okay if this kind of "get on board" behavior has not exactly been your brand in the past. People are allowed to change. You are allowed to "see the light." Almost every time you hear about a change, the train has left the station and is picking up speed. You will be best served if you get on the train and try to move to the front and drive the train if you can. You can also choose to leave the station and try to find a different train, but don't stand on the track or otherwise try to stop the train. You will get run over and the train will barely notice.

"The Future You"—Last Looks

As a leader, there exists the opportunity for You to make Us better. You can begin to make your team, and possibly your company, a better place to work, an organization that better serves its customers and clients, a company that finds ways to do better with social and environmental responsibility, to be better at the things that are important to both you and the company—that's Us. Whether it's with your boss or your team, either as a leader or as one of the group, working together makes things better. There aren't that many leadership jobs so take it as a golden opportunity to thoughtfully, carefully, and profitably make things better.

We aren't leadership experts. We didn't study leadership at an Ivy League business school. We haven't given leadership seminars, written leadership papers, or penned *NY Times* bestsellers on the topic of leadership. We learned leadership in the school of hard knocks. We learned leadership by doing; sometimes we failed and sometimes we succeeded. We probably learned more from our failures than our successes, but the common denominator of both is that we learned and worked to get better. Our thoughts on leadership are intended to help you figure out where you can get better. We want our leadership failures, our pain, to be your gain. We want the leadership success stories to similarly inspire you to work on your leadership skills. We want you to take full advantage of your leadership opportunity when it comes your way. Like Seals and Crofts (a 70s duo) sang, "We may never pass this way again." Each leadership opportunity is unique, and you are unlikely to get a second chance at that specific opportunity. So take it as a precious opportunity and do all You can possibly do to make Us better.

You can learn to be a leader. You have to want it. You have to learn to be comfortable being uncomfortable. You have to choose a continuous improvement mindset. You can do all of those things and you can change the world by starting to lead positive change right where you are planted; right now, in your company in the leadership opportunity you have in front of you. Go forth and prosper! You will make Us better.

Afterword

THE JOURNEY TO COMPLETE OUR FIRST BOOK HAS BEEN A LONG AND winding road. From our first lunch meeting to discuss the idea of a book, at the typical lunch place in the typical suburban mall, through multiple edits and rewrites to a version that we are now proud to present to you. The journey is a big part of the learning experience and so it was with our book. It certainly made us better writers and communicators. It was really the questions and the comments ("What are you trying to say?" "Is that really the right word?" "Wow, that's so negative!," and our all-time favorite, "Dude, you know that makes no sense!!") that caused us to take a critical look at what we were doing. We really had to better illuminate our stories and sharpen the points we were making. We had to get over ourselves.

The journey also led us to reconsider how we were behaving along the way. We had to look closely at our own advice lest we became our own Klown Kar. We had to reset our mindset towards criticism, advice, mentoring, and quality. The end result is that we worked together to produce a mélange of stories and advice that really impacted us and stuck in our memories, culled from every decade of our corporate existence. Our corporate experience spans the decades from President Jimmy Carter to whoever is in the White House today, and the lessons learned at the advent of our careers hold true today as they did when gas was less than a buck a gallon.

Yes, the world has changed since those days. Some of those changes are for the better and some aren't. Concepts such as loyalty, performance,

161

compensation, benefits and career are different today than they were and they will continue to evolve over time as technology evolves and culture adapts. We sought to focus on those elements of You and Them that really aren't changing and those are the more "human" elements. Those are the aspects of Corporate America that truly exist in the intersection of You and Them—they are about Us. As we look back at our own careers and look forward to continuing to work and be productive members of society, we find we were the most productive and the happiest when we figured out what Us really meant and operated in that zone. We hope you can find this happy place as well.

Acknowledgments

THERE ARE MANY PEOPLE TO THANK BECAUSE THIS IS A JOURNEY THAT requires an entourage. We have to start with our wives who read our text and offered us loving, respectful and excellent comments, listened to us read edited and rewritten chapters in which we took particular individual pride and let us prattle on about the editing and publishing processes. Thank you Connie and Johanna—you know we love you!!

David asked his adult sons (Joel, Paul, Mark, and Andrew) to join him behind the proverbial curtain and they offered encouragement, advice and some great editorial suggestions all the while keeping him humble as they have sworn to do as part of the universal Father/Son Pact. One of David's nephews, Kevin, read a few pages about the Unwritten Rules about two months after he started his first job out of college and he offered what was the greatest bit of encouragement, "Hey Man, can I please get the rest of the book." Much love and respect to all of you.

Simon's children, who are still in their high school and early college years as we finish this book, have mostly been working on their eye-rolls and glazed looks as Dad tries in vain to convey the wisdom we've put together in this book and assure them of how helpful all of these tips will be for them someday. Maybe they will at least see value in David's stories!

Thank you to our friends and work colleagues with whom we shared portions of our book. Your comments and advice were useful and inspiring. We added a few items to the book because of you and are grateful for your friendship. We worked with a couple of editors one of whom wanted to create artificial personas for us (we had to be true to ourselves—couldn't do this) and the other who gave us a great copy edit a couple of drafts before we really needed it (a bit like bringing the Closer in to pitch the sixth inning of a baseball game). While they didn't help us get this across the finish line, they did help us with the book and we appreciate their efforts.

Our efforts really came together with the help of Dr. Patricia Ross at Hugo House Publishers. She helped us think through ways to better organize our advice, better tell our stories, and better make our points. Simply put, she helped make the book better and actually enabled us to take it across the finish line—yes, holding hands! We will be forever grateful for her efforts and contagious enthusiasm and support. Thank you Patricia.

We don't know the future. We can't tell you what's in store for you. We can't tell you what long and winding literary journeys await us. There will be more journeys. We look forward to continuing on as life-long learners and teachers, and we wish the same for you.

About the Authors

DAVID HARRISON has more than forty years of experience in the engineering and construction industry with a focus on water and wastewater systems. He has worked on projects across the United States, in Australia, and in the United Kingdom for municipal government agencies and private industry. He is a registered professional engineer in the State of California and a Board-Certified Environmental Engineer, but he is also an unusual engineer as he seems to be a mid-level extrovert. Mr. Harrison's experience also includes executive-level positions in the marketing and sales of professional services service. He served as Director of Client Service and then Director of Marketing for North America for MWH, a global water engineering and construction company. Mr. Harrison is currently a Vice President and Director of Program Management Services for Kennedy Jenks Consultants, a North American engineering and technology consultancy. He has written extensively on the topic of client service for professional services practices.

Mr. Harrison has a BS in Civil Engineering from UC Davis and an MS in Environmental Engineering from Stanford. He and his wife Connie have been married for more than forty years. They have four adult sons and three mostly perfect grandchildren. He enjoys road cycling, reading, music and sports and is always happy to engage in a healthy debate on these topics or the tangible business applications of any episode of *The Office*.

SIMON HEART has thirty-plus years of experience surviving and thriving in corporate America. Working in large companies and small, doing business internationally and in nearly every U.S. state, and holding nearly every job on the corporate ladder from summer intern to CEO, Mr. Heart has spent his career as both a student of and a participant in what it takes to succeed in a corporation. Beyond his personal career experiences, Mr. Heart spent two decades in the management consulting arena managing teams and helping individuals and organizations understand what it takes to succeed and how best to reach their personal and organizational goals. Mr. Heart is the founder and CEO of Heart Enterprises Inc., which offers real estate investment and property management solutions for hundreds of property owners in Northern Colorado as part of the All County Property Management franchise network.

Mr. Heart has a B.A. in Environmental Sciences from Wesleyan University and an M.S. in Environmental Engineering from the University of California at Berkeley. He lives with his wife Johanna and their three children Isabella, Eli, and Zoe, in Boulder, Colorado.

If you're looking for more ...

We are available to speak with your group, your team, your graduating class—you name it. We've got lots more stories and are always interested in meeting new people, talking about topics of interest to your group and answering questions—even the tough ones.

We are available for small or large group facilitation and key notes. We also offer one-on-one or group coaching and weekend retreats. Our goal is to inspire people to realize their potential, achieve work-life balance, and set themselves up for a successful career in corporate America.

Find out if we are the right fit for your group!

You can reach us at **www.RightStartBook.com**. All speeches and workshops are tailored to your issues and concerns.

Let us know what's on your mind and we'll figure out how to make things work.

CPSIA information can be obtained
at www.ICGtesting.com
Printed in the USA
LVHW090130010720
659431LV00005B/1143

9 781948 261357